Microsoft Power[barcode obscures text]
(Microsoft 365 Apps and Office 2019)
Introduction and Certification Study Guide

Daniel John Stine

SDC
PUBLICATIONS

SDC Publications
P.O. Box 1334
Mission, KS 66222
913-262-2664
www.SDCpublications.com
Publisher: Stephen Schroff

ISBN-13: 978-1-63057-500-7
ISBN-10: 1-63057-500-3

Printed and bound in the United States of America.

Foreword

<u>Intended audience</u>
Created for students and professionals, this book teaches the use of PowerPoint to create well formatted, high-quality presentations. Additionally, anyone interested in practicing for the Microsoft PowerPoint (Microsoft 365 Apps and Office 2019) certification exam will also benefit.

<u>Introduction</u>
This book provides a collection of study materials to both learn PowerPoint and to prepare for the Microsoft PowerPoint (Microsoft 365 Apps and Office 2019) Exam (Exam MO-300). With a range of options for most learning styles, this book will help improve your skill level and provide an additional boost of confidence, which is sure to increase the chances of a successful exam outcome.

Study material for all learning styles, including:

📖 Printed book
- o **Introduction to PowerPoint** *with no previous experience required*
- o **Focused Study** *on objective domains*
- o **Flashcards** *cut out with scissors*
- o **Exam Day Study Guide** *one page reference*

⬇ Downloads
- o **Narrated Videos** *with optional captions*
- o **Practice Software** *Prerequisite: Microsoft PowerPoint 365/2019 installed*

The book begins with an overview of the user interface and then dives into the following categories in more detail:
- Manage Presentations
- Manage Slides
- Insert and Format Text, Shapes, and Images
- Insert Tables, Charts, SmartArt, 3D Models, and Media
- Apply Transitions and Animations

The text concludes with an overview of the included practice exam software download. This software mimics the real exam as much as possible, in terms of user interface, number and types of questions, as well as a time constraint. While this study guide cannot claim to cover every possible question that may arise in the exam, it does help to firm up your basic knowledge to positively deal with most questions… thus, leaving more time to reflect on the more difficult questions.

<u>Two books in one</u>

- Introduction to PowerPoint for beginners
  No previous experience is required to use this book to learn Microsoft PowerPoint. This book is focused on the basics and building a solid foundation. But, even if you have some experience with PowerPoint, the book offers valuable tips and workflows.

- Certification exam study guide
  In addition to learning PowerPoint, this book is also geared towards those wishing to formalize the conclusion of their learning experience by taking the Microsoft PowerPoint (Microsoft 365 Apps and Office 2019) certification exam.

> **Errata:**
> Please check the publisher's website from time to time for any errors or typos found once printed. Simply browse to www.SDCpublications.com, and then navigate to the page for this book. Click the **View/Submit errata** link in the upper right corner of the page. If you find an error, please submit it so we can correct it in the next edition.
>
> You may contact the publisher with comments or suggestions at service@SDCpublications.com.

About the Author:

Daniel John Stine AIA, IES, CSI, CDT, is a registered architect (WI) with over twenty years of experience in the field of architecture. He has worked on many multi-million-dollar projects, including a nearly $1 billion dollar hospital project in the Midwest. Throughout these years of professional practice, Stine has leveraged many of the Microsoft Office products to organize, manage, and present on large complex projects.

He has presented internationally on architecture and design technology in the USA, Canada, Ireland, Scotland, Denmark, Slovenia, Australia and Singapore; and has been a top-rated speaker on several occasions. By invitation, in 2016, he spent a week at Autodesk's largest R&D facility in Shanghai, China, to beta test and brainstorm new features in their flagship architectural design software, Revit.

Committed to furthering the design profession, Stine teaches graduate architecture students at North Dakota State University (NDSU) and has lectured for design programs at NDSU, Northern Iowa State, University of Minnesota, University of Texas at San Antonio (UTSA), as well as Dunwoody's new School of Architecture in Minneapolis. As an adjunct instructor, Dan previously taught AutoCAD and Revit for twelve years at Lake Superior College. He is a member of the American Institute of Architects (AIA), Construction Specifications Institute (CSI), Autodesk Developer Network (ADN), Autodesk Expert Elite, and is a Construction Document Technician (issued by CSI).

In addition to Microsoft Office certification study guides, Stine has written multiple books on architectural design software, all written using Microsoft Word and published by SDC Publications.

You may contact the publisher with comments or suggestions at service@SDCpublications.com.

Table of Contents

1. Manage Presentations

2. Manage Slides

3. Insert and Format Text, Shapes, and Images

4. Insert Tables, Charts, SmartArt, 3D Models, and Media

5. Apply Transitions and Animations

6. Practice Exam (Provided with this Book)

7. Certification Study Resources

7.1.1 **Exam Day Study Guide**: one page

7.2.1 **Flashcards**: 50 cards

Index

Included Online Resources

Online resources may be download from SDC Publications using access code and instructions on the inside-front cover of this book.

 Practice Exam Software: Test your skills with this included resource

Videos: 85 short, narrated videos covering each exam outcome

0 Getting Started

0.0 Getting Started

Before you can begin learning the ins and outs of PowerPoint, you need to open it up.

0.0.0 Starting PowerPoint

Here are the main ways to start PowerPoint. Adding the PowerPoint icon to the taskbar, at the bottom of the screen, is the most efficient but it is not there by default.

1. Click the **Start Menu**
2. Select **PowerPoint** from the list
3. Two additional options:
   a. Type "PowerPoint" in the **search**, select PowerPoint in the search results list.
   b. Most efficient: Right-click on the PowerPoint icon in step #2, select "Pin to taskbar," single-click new icon on **taskbar** to start PowerPoint.

Starting PowerPoint

0.1 User Interface

PowerPoint is a powerful and sophisticated program. Because of its powerful feature set, it has a measurable learning curve. However, like anything, when broken down into smaller pieces, we can easily learn to harness the power of PowerPoint.

Next, we will walk through the different aspects of the User Interface (UI). As with any program, understanding the user interface, and correct terminology, is the key to using the program's features, and using this study guide efficiently.

Backstage Screen

When PowerPoint is first opened, the Backstage screen is presented, as shown in the image below. Clicking the **Blank Presentation** tile (i.e. template) is the quickest way to get working in PowerPoint. Use the **Open** option or **Recent/Pinned** files options to access existing PowerPoint files. To verify User or Product information use the **Account** command in the lower left. Finally, the **Options** command opens the same-named dialog with a plethora of settings and options to control PowerPoint's default behavior.

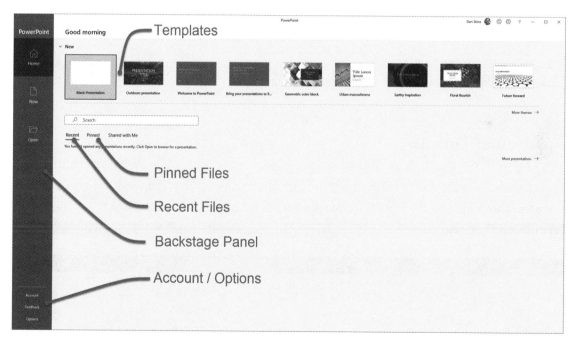

PowerPoint Home Screen

The image below highlights important terms to know for the PowerPoint user interface.

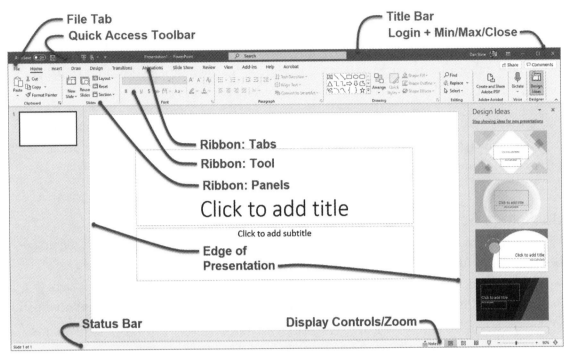

PowerPoint User Interface

Now, let's take a closer look at some aspects of the User Interface.

Application Title Bar

In addition to the *Quick Access Toolbar* and application controls, which are covered in the next few sections, you are also presented with the product name (PowerPoint) and the current file **name** in the center on the Application Title bar. The Search bar can be used to quickly find features and get help.

File Tab

Access to Backstage tools such as *New, Open, Save, Save As, Share, Export, Print,* and more. You also have access to tools which control the PowerPoint application as a whole, not just the current presentation, such as *Options* (see the end of this section for more on *Options*).

To exit the Backstage and return to your presentation, click the left-pointing arrow in the upper left, as pointed out below.

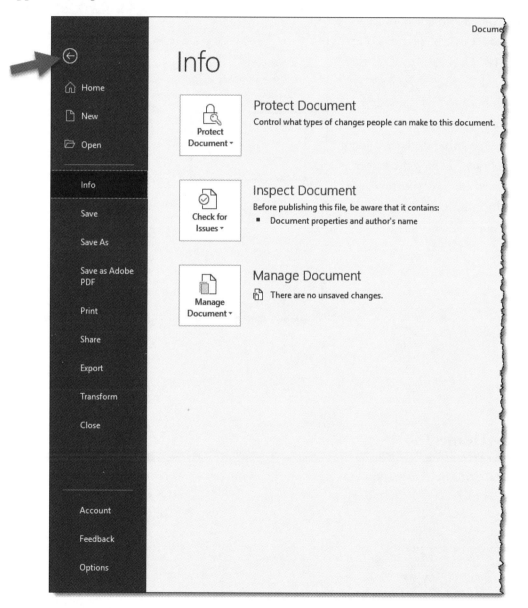

Quick Access Toolbar

Referred to as *QAT* in this book, this single toolbar provides access to often used tools: *AutoSave, Save, Undo, Redo.*

These tools are always quickly accessible, regardless of what part of the *Ribbon* is active.

The *QAT* can be positioned above or below the *Ribbon* and any command from the *Ribbon* can be placed on it; simply right-click on any tool on the *Ribbon* and select *Add to Quick Access Toolbar.* Moving the *QAT* below the *Ribbon* gives you a lot more room for your favorite commands to be added from the *Ribbon.* Clicking the larger down-arrow to the far right reveals a list of common tools which can be toggled on and off (see image to right).

Ribbon – Home Tab

The *Home* tab, on the *Ribbon,* contains most of the common PowerPoint formatting & basic manipulation tools.

The *Ribbon* has three types of buttons: *button, drop-down button* and *split button.*

In the two following images, you can see the *Replace* tool is a **split button**. Most of the time you would simply click the main part of the button to search for text in the current document. Clicking the down-arrow part of the button, for the *Find* tool example, gives you additional options: Advanced Find and Go To….

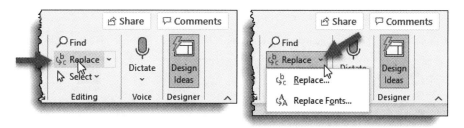

The next image is an example of a **drop-down button**. For this example, there is no dominant Select option provided. Rather, we are always required to select from a list.

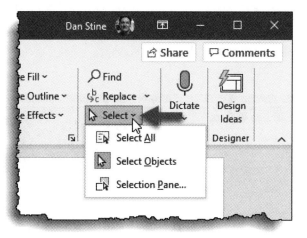

Ribbon – Insert Tab

To view this tab, simply click the label "Insert" near the top of the *Ribbon*. Notice that the current tab is underlined. This tab presents a series of tools which allow you to insert objects, images and more into the current presentation.

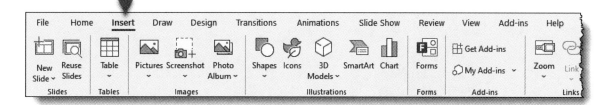

Ribbon – Slide Show Tab

The Slide Show tab controls the way the presentation is displayed during the formal presentation.

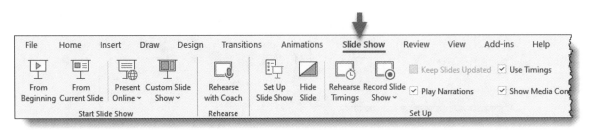

Clicking a "Start Slide Show" option takes over your entire screen (or both screens if you have two monitors). To exit this mode, click the Esc key or the END SLIDE SHOW command shown below (the latter is on a dual screen setup). The DISPLAY SETTINGS list allows the presentation to be swapped to the other screen.

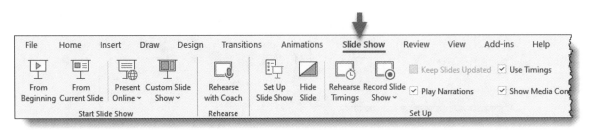

Ribbon – View Tab

The tools on the *View* tab allow you to toggle the Ruler and Gridlines on and off. Here you can also change the view mode (e.g. Reading, Notes Page, Outline, etc.) and zoom the current presentation.

Ribbon – Add-in Tabs

If you install an **add-in** for PowerPoint on your computer, you will likely see a new tab appear on the Ribbon. Some add-ins are free while others require a fee. The image below shows two popular PDF writer/editor tools installed: Bluebeam and Adobe Acrobat.

Ribbon Visibility

The *Ribbon* can be displayed in one of two states:

- Full Ribbon (default)
- Minimize to Tabs

The intent of this feature is to increase the size of the available work area, which is helpful when using a tablet or laptop with a smaller display. It is recommended, however, that you leave the *Ribbon* fully expanded while learning to use the program. The images in this book show the fully expanded state. When using the minimized option, simply click on a Tab to temporarily reveal the tools. Click the Pin icon in the lower right to lock it open.

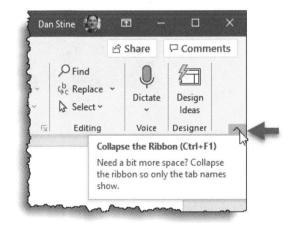

FYI: Double-clicking on a Ribbon tab will also toggle the Ribbon visibility.

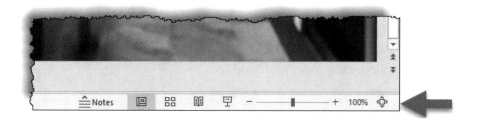

Minimized to Tabs

Temporarily Expanded

When using a tablet or touch screen, a Draw tab will also appear on the Ribbon.

Status Bar

This area will display the current slide number, total number of slides, in the current presentation.

The right-hand side of the *Status Bar* shows the current zoom level and four view mode toggles: **Normal** (default), **Slide Sorter**, **Reading View**, and **Slide Show**. The **Notes** icon toggles the notes pane. Finally, if the Zoom level has been manually adjusted, clicking the **Fit Slide to Current Window** icon on the far right will reset the Zoom level to match the size of the current window on screen (which is the default setting).

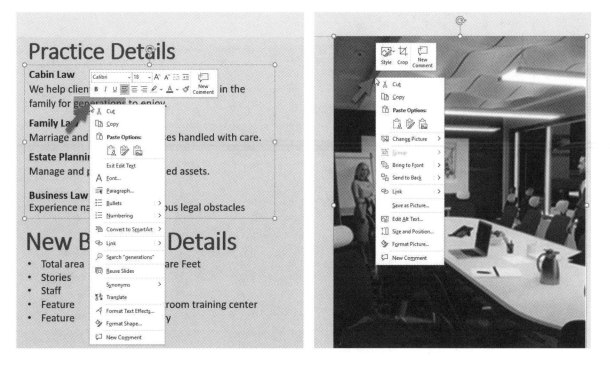

Hover your cursor over an icon for the tool name and a brief description of what it does as shown in the image to the left. Notice, there is also a link to the Help documentation via the **Tell me more** option.

Context Menu

The *context menu* appears near the cursor whenever you **right-click** on the mouse. The options on that menu will vary depending on what is selected, as shown in the two examples below (text selected on the left, an image on the right). Notice, the formatting toolbar also appears, facilitating quick adjustments, such as making text bold or a different color.

PowerPoint Options

The Options dialog, accessed from the File tab, has a significant number of settings, toggles and options used to modify how the program works. It is recommended that you don't make any changes here right now. The certification exam will be based on the default settings.

Efficient Practices

The *Ribbon* and menus are helpful when learning a program like PowerPoint; however, many experienced users rarely use them! The process of moving the mouse to the edge of the screen to select a command and then back to where you were is very inefficient, especially for those who do this all day long, five days a week. Here are a few ways experienced PowerPoint operators work:

- Use the **Wheel** on the mouse to scroll vertically and hold the **Ctrl key** while spinning the wheel to zoom in and out.

- PowerPoint conforms to many of the Microsoft Windows operating system standards. Most programs, including PowerPoint, have several standard commands that can be accessed via keyboard shortcuts. Here are a few examples (press both keys at the same time):

o	Ctrl + S	Save	*Saves the current file*
o	Ctrl + A	Select All	*Selects everything*
o	Ctrl + Z	Undo	*Undoes the previous action*
o	Ctrl + X	Cut	*Cut to Windows clipboard*
o	Ctrl + C	Copy	*Copy to selected content to the clipboard*
o	Ctrl + V	Paste	*Paste clipboard contents at cursor location*
o	Ctrl + P	Print	*Opens print dialog*
o	Ctrl + N	New	*Create new file*
o	F7	Spelling	*Launch spell check feature*

- Many PowerPoint commands also have keyboard shortcuts. Hover your cursor over a button to see its tooltip and shortcut (if it has one). In the example shown below, press **Ctrl + M** to insert a slide into the presentation.

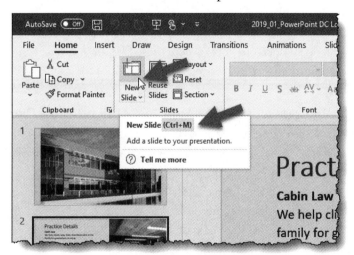

Keyboard shortcut on tooltip

This concludes your brief overview of the PowerPoint user interface.

0.2 Certification Introduction

In the competitive world in which we live it is important to stand out to potential employers and prove your capabilities. One way to do this is by passing one of the Microsoft Certification Exams. A candidate who passes an exam has credentials from the makers of the software that you know how to use their software. This can help employers narrow down the list of potential interviewees when searching for candidates and reviewing resumes.

When the exam is successfully passed a certificate may be printed and displayed at your desk or included with your resume. You also have access to a Microsoft badge for use on business cards or on flyers promoting your work.

The exams <u>are</u> based on a specific release of PowerPoint. It is important that you ensure your version of PowerPoint matches the version covered in this book, and the version of the exam you wish to take. Ideally, you will want to take the exam for the newest version to prove you have the current skills needed in today's competitive workforce.

Important Things to Know

Here are a few big picture things you should keep in mind:

- **Practice Exam**
  - The practice exam, that comes with this book, is taken on **your own computer**
  - You need to have **PowerPoint installed** and ready to use during the practice exam
  - You must download the practice exam software from SDC Publications
    - See inside-front cover of this book for access instructions
  - **Required files** for the practice test
    - Files are downloaded with practice exam software
    - You do not need to know where these files are located
  - Note which questions you got wrong, and study those topics

- **Microsoft PowerPoint (Microsoft 365 Apps and Office 2019) - Exam**
  - Purchase the **exam voucher** ahead of time
    - If you buy it the day of the test, or at the test center, there may be an issue with the voucher showing up in your account
    - Note: some testing locations charge an extra proctoring fee.
  - Make a **reservation** at a test center; walk-ins are not allowed
  - A computer is provided at the test center
  - Have your Certiport **username** and **password** memorized (or written down)
  - If you fail, note which sections you had trouble with and study those topics
  - You must wait 24 hours before retaking the exam

Benefits

There are a variety of reasons and benefits to getting certified. They range from a school/employer requirement to professional development and resume building. Whatever the reason, there is really no downside to this effort.

Here are some of the benefits:

- Earn an industry-recognized credential that helps prove your skill level and can get you hired.
- Develop your skills with sample projects and exercises that emphasize real-world applications.
- Accelerate your professional development and help enhance your credibility and career success.
- Boost academic performance, prepare for the demands of a job, and open doors to career opportunities.
- Display your Microsoft certificate, use the Microsoft Certified badge, highlight your achievement and get noticed.

Certificate

When the exam is successfully passed, a certificate signed by Microsoft's CEO is issued with your name on it. This can be framed and displayed at your desk, copied and included with a resume (if appropriate) or brought to an interview (not the framed version, just a copy!).

Badging

In addition to a certificate, a badge is issued. Badging is a digital web-enabled version of your credential by **Acclaim**, which can be helpful to potential employers. This is a quick proof that you know how to use the PowerPoint features covered by the 365/2019 Associate exam.

Certified Specialist, Expert *and* Master

While this study guide focuses solely on the **PowerPoint Associate** exam, it is helpful to know about the other options for future consideration. There are seven different exam options. These are all paid options, not free, but when considering the value outlined previously, it is worth it. See the links at the end of this section to learn more about costs.

Associate	Expert	Master
Excel	Excel Expert - - - - - - - - - - - - -▶	Excel Expert
PowerPoint*	PowerPoint Expert - - - - - - - -▶	PowerPoint Expert
PowerPoint -▶		PowerPoint
Access		Access *or* Outlook
Outlook		

* = Covered in this book

Microsoft PowerPoint (Microsoft 365 Apps and Office 2019) certification

Microsoft PowerPoint (Microsoft 365 Apps and Office 2019) certification is an excellent way for students and professionals to validate their software skills.

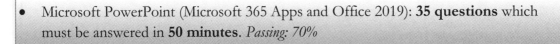

- Microsoft PowerPoint (Microsoft 365 Apps and Office 2019): **35 questions** which must be answered in **50 minutes**. *Passing: 70%*

Additional Microsoft Office certifications

In addition to the Microsoft PowerPoint (Microsoft 365 Apps and Office 2019) certification, which this study guide is based on, these are the other options and their format.

- Excel: There are 35 questions which must be answered in 50 minutes.
- Word: There are 35 questions which must be answered in 50 minutes.
- Excel Expert: There are 25 questions which must be answered in 50 minutes.
- Word Expert: There are 25 questions which must be answered in 50 minutes.
- Access: There are 31 questions which must be answered in 50 minutes.
- Outlook: There are 35 questions which must be answered in 50 minutes.

A special "Master" designation is earned if **both Expert** (PowerPoint & Excel) are passed along with the **Outlook** and **PowerPoint** *or* **Access** exams.

All exams are live in-the-application style questions.

Exam Topics and Objectives

The Microsoft PowerPoint (Microsoft 365 Apps and Office 2019) exam covers six main topics. The outline below lists the specific topics one needs to be familiar with to pass the test. The remainder of this book expounds upon each of these items. In fact, this is the outline for each of the remaining chapters.

1. **Manage Presentations**
   - Modify slide masters, handout masters, and note masters
   - Change presentation options and views
   - Configure print settings for presentations
   - Configure and present slide shows
   - Prepare presentations for collaboration

2. **Manage Slides**
   - Insert slides
   - Modify slides
   - Order and group slides

3. **Insert and Format Text, Shapes, and Images**
   - Format text
   - Insert links

   - Insert and format images
   - Insert and format graphic elements
   - Order and group objects on slides

4. **Insert Tables, Charts, SmartArt, 3D Models, and Media**
   - Insert and format tables
   - Insert and modify charts
   - Insert and format SmartArt graphics
   - Insert and modify 3D models
   - Insert and manage media

5. **Apply Transitions and Animations**
   - Apply and configure slide transitions
   - Animate slide content
   - Set timing for transitions

Exam Releases (including languages)

The **Certiport** website lists which languages and units of measure the exam & practice tests are available in as partially shown in the image below. For the full list, follow this link: https://certiport.pearsonvue.com/Educator-resources/Exam-details/Exam-releases

Microsoft Office Specialist (MOS)

✓+ = Recently Released ✓ = Released
"Date" = Planned Release Date
"Blank" = Unavailable/Undetermined
"GMetrix" or "MeasureUp" = Practice test
Note: You may need to scroll right to see all of the languages.

MOS (Microsoft 365 Apps and Office 2019) Exams   MOS 2016 Exams   MOS 2013 Exams

Microsoft Office Specialist (Microsoft 365 Apps and Office 2019) Exams

	Product	ENU	ARA	CHS	CHT	DEU	ELL	ESM	FRA	IND	ITA	JPN	KOR	MAY	NLD	PLK	PTI
Word	Exam	✓+	✓+	✓+	✓+	✓+	✓+	✓+	✓+	✓+	✓+	✓+	✓+	✓+	✓+	✓+	✓+
	GMetrix	✓+	✓+		✓+	✓+	✓+	✓+	✓+	✓+	✓+		✓+		✓+		✓+
Excel	Exam	✓+	✓+	✓+	✓+	✓+	✓+	✓+	✓+	✓+	✓+	✓+	✓+	✓+	✓+	✓+	✓+
	GMetrix	✓+	✓+		✓+	✓+	✓+	✓+	✓+	✓+			✓+		✓+		✓+
PowerPoint	Exam	✓+	✓+	✓+	✓+	✓+	✓+	✓+	✓+	✓+	✓+	✓+	✓+	✓+	✓+	✓+	✓+
	GMetrix	✓+	✓+		✓+	✓+	✓+	✓+	✓+	✓+			✓+		✓+		✓+
Outlook	Exam	✓+	✓+	✓+	✓+	✓+		✓+	✓+			✓+	✓+		✓+		
	GMetrix	✓+		Jun	Jun			✓+									
Word Expert	Exam	✓+		✓+	✓+	✓+		✓+	✓+			✓+	✓+				

Exam releases

Certified Training Centers

To find the nearest testing center, start here: http://portal.certiport.com/Locator

Unfortunately, there may not be a test center in your city. In this case, you will have to plan a day to travel to the testing center to take the exam. In this case it is much more important to have made an appointment, purchased the voucher ahead of time and associated it with your Certiport account… and of course, studied the material well, so you do not have to retake it.

Locating a training center

From the **Certiport** frequently Asked Questions (FAQ) online page:

> If schools or districts want to run exams onsite, they can easily become a testing center and run the exams seamlessly in class. Institutions can sign up to be centers on the Certiport site."

Practice Exam (included with this book)

Practice exam software is included with this book which can be downloaded from the publisher's website using the **access code** found on the inside-front cover. This is a good way to check your skills prior to taking the official exam, as the intent is to offer similar types of questions in roughly the same format as the official exam. This practice exam is taken at home, work or school, on your own computer. You must have PowerPoint installed and access to the provided sample files, to successfully answer the in-application questions.

This is a test drive for the exam process:

- Understanding the test software
- How to mark and return to questions
- Exam question format
- Live in-application steps
- How the results are presented at the exam conclusion

An example of the PowerPoint practice exam is shown in the image below. When the practice exam software is started, PowerPoint is also opened and positioned directly above. During the timed exam seven projects are presented, each consisting of a separate PowerPoint file in which five questions must be answered by modifying the current PowerPoint document. At the end, the practice exam software will grade and present the results for the exam.

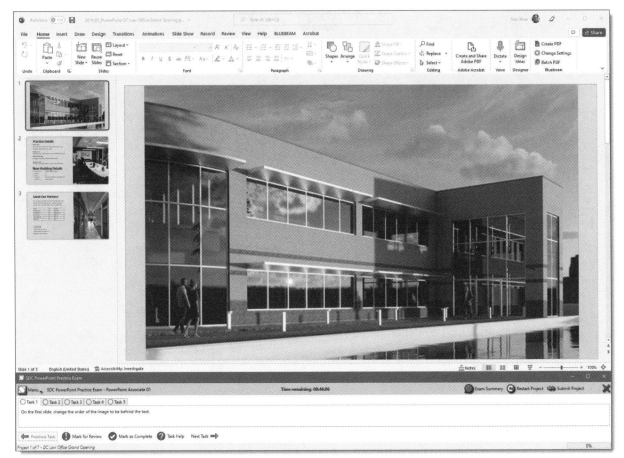

Included Practice Exam Software Example

Having taken the practice exam can remove some anxiety one may have going into an exam that may positively impact your career search.

See chapter 7 for more details on the Practice Exam software provided with this book.

Exam Preparation

Before taking the exam, you can prepare by working through **this study guide** and then the **practice exam**. You may also want to drive to the test location a day or so before the exam to make sure you know where it is and what the parking options are (if driving yourself) to ensure you are on time the day of the exam.

During the Exam

During the exam, be sure to manage your time. Quickly go through the test and answer the questions that are easy to you, skipping the ones you are not immediately sure of. The exam software allows you to view a list of questions you have not answered or have marked. Once you have answered all the easy questions you can then go back and think through those which remain. Do not exit the exam until you are completely finished, as you will not be able to re-enter the exam after that point.

 During the exam, some PowerPoint functionality is disabled, such as Help.

Exam Results

Once the exam is finished you will receive notification of your score immediately. You must earn 700 points (out of 1000) to pass, but this is a scaled score based on weighted questions. Thus, 70% does not exactly equal a passing score. If you failed, you should note the objective areas you were not as strong in and study those areas more before taking the test again – see image below. Be sure to print your score report and take it with you to study – it is also possible to log into your Certiport account later and print it from home.

SECTION ANALYSIS	
Manage Presentations	75%
Manage Slides	100%
Insert and Format Text, Shapes, and Images	100%
Insert Tables, Charts, SmartArt, 3D Models, and Media	100%
Apply Transitions and Animations	100%

FINAL SCORE	
Required Score	700
Your Score	945

OUTCOME	
Pass	✓

Retaking the Exam

If the exam is failed, don't worry as you can take it again – as soon as 24 hours later. If you have any doubt about your ability to easily pass the exam, consider purchasing a voucher that includes a reduced cost "retake" option.

In the event that you do not pass the exam, and you have purchased the retake option, a retake code will be emailed to you. You may re-take the exam after waiting 24 hours from the time your initial exam was first started. Retake vouchers must be used within 60 days of the failed exam.

Here is the currently posted retake policy for the certification exam:

- If a candidate does not achieve a passing score on an exam the first time, the candidate must wait 24 hours before retaking the exam.
- If a candidate does not achieve a passing score the second time, the candidate must wait 2 days (48 hours) before retaking the exam a third time.
- A two-day waiting period will be imposed for each subsequent exam retake.
- There is no annual limit on the number of attempts on the same exam.
- If a candidate achieves a passing score on an MOS exam, the candidate may take it again.
- Test results found to be in violation of this retake policy will result in the candidate not being awarded the attempted credential, regardless of score.

Resources

For more information visit these sites:

- Certiport:
  https://certiport.pearsonvue.com/Certifications/Microsoft/MOS/Overview
- Acclaim (Credly):
  https://www.youracclaim.com/
- Microsoft:
  https://www.microsoft.com/en-us/learning/certification-exam-policies.aspx

Certiport User Registration

Here are the steps to create a Certiport account, which is required to take the exam.

Start here: https://www.certiport.com/Portal/Pages/Registration.aspx

Follow the steps outlined on the site. Once complete, you will be prompted to register your account with a certification program. **Important:** be sure to select the Microsoft option in this step, and not Autodesk, Adobe, etc. This is done on the **Program tab** per the image below, just click the **Register** button (to the right of Microsoft) to get started.

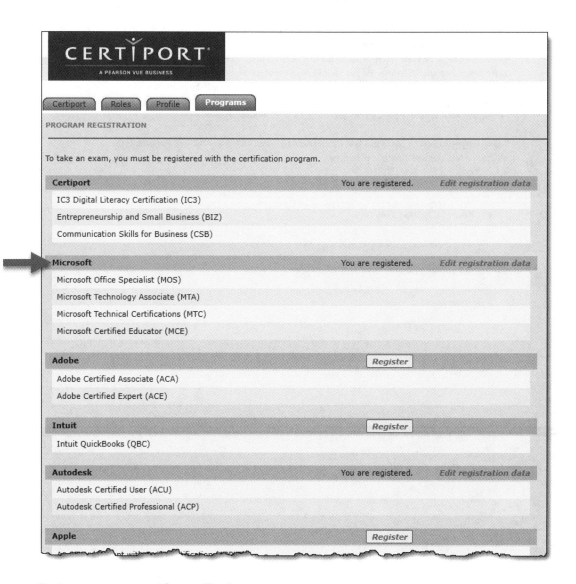

Register your account with a certification program

Once you click Register, you will be prompted to verify your personal information on a new page. Once you complete this information and click Finish you will receive a confirmation email stating you are enrolled in the Microsoft certification program like the one shown below.

Registration confirmation email from Certiport

1 Manage Presentations

Introduction

Review essential aspects of PowerPoint: navigation, formatting, saving and inspecting documents.

1.0 Create presentations

The process of learning how to use Microsoft PowerPoint starts with opening the application, which was covered in the previous chapter, and then creating a new document. This section covers the steps required to create a new document.

1.0.0 From templates

The most common way to start a new document is from a template. A template is a special version of a PowerPoint presentation with specific settings, such as margins, spacing, etc. It can also have text and graphics. For example, it might have a company name and logo for a common sales template. The main thing to know about a template is that when opened, via the New command, a copy of the document is what is opened. This prevents the template from getting altered unintentionally.

Create a new presentation from a template:

1. Open PowerPoint (covered in the previous chapter)
2. Select a template:
    a. Click a template shown across the top, Blank presentation is most common
    b. Or, Click More Themes to see more purpose-specific options
3. Save the new presentation
    a. Provide a file location and name

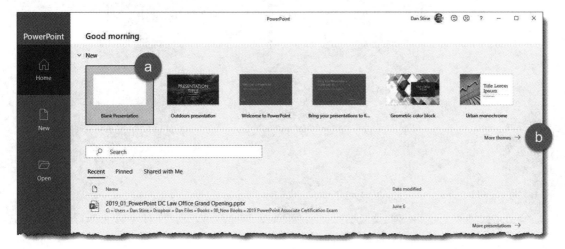

Create new presentation from template

1.0.1 From right-click in File Explorer

It is possible to create a new presentation outside of PowerPoint, within File Explorer. This method uses the Blank document template.

> **Tip:** An easy way to open Microsoft Windows **File Explorer** is by the following keystrokes on the keyboard: **Windows key + E** (just press the two keys at the same time).

Create a new presentation from right-clicking within File Explorer:

1. Within File Explorer, **right-click** in a blank area within a folder.
2. Click **New** in the menu.
3. Select **Microsoft PowerPoint Presentation**
   a. Provide a file name

Create new presentation from right-click in File Explorer

File extensions:

When opening PowerPoint presentations, looking at its files on your computer, or preparing to copy them, it is helpful to know what the two *main* file extensions are.

- PowerPoint document   filename.**pptx**
- PowerPoint template   filename.**potm**
- Legacy document   filename.ppt ('97 – 2003)
- Legacy template   filename.pot ('97 – 2003)

Note: By default, file extensions may not be showing within **File Explorer**. If desired, they may be turned on within File Explorer via View (tab) → Options → Change folder and search options → View (tab in dialog) → (uncheck) Hide extensions for known file types.

1.1 Modify slide masters, handout masters, and note masters

Knowing how to navigate within a document is important for efficiency and accuracy.

1.1.0 Open existing presentations

Here are the steps to return to a previously created presentation.

Open an existing presentation:

1. Start PowerPoint, and then click **Open** on the left panel
2. Click **Browse**
3. In the Open dialog, browse to your presentation location, and **select it**
4. Click **Open**

Open a previously created presentation

1.1.1 Change the slide master theme or background

The slide master for each presentation controls the look of the content, but not the content itself. The theme and/or background may be changed at any time; however, some formatting might be required due to font size changes.

Change the master slide theme:

The theme changes all background settings: colors, fonts, effects, and background Styles.

1. On the View tab, select **Master Slide**
2. From the **Themes** drop-down, select the desired theme
3. Click **Close Master View**

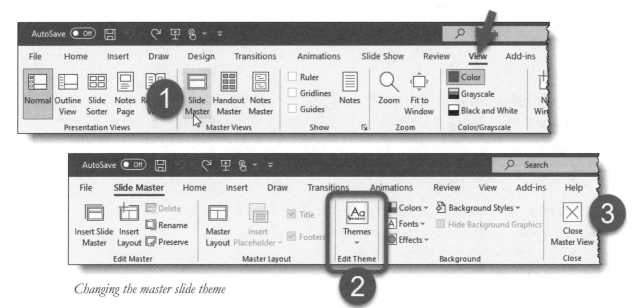

Changing the master slide theme

Change the master slide background:

For quick adjustments, background settings may be changed apart from the theme.

1. On the View tab, select **Master Slide**
2. From the **Background** panel, adjust one or more of the following:
    a. **Colors**: coordinated palette of colors for text, lists, lines, etc.
    b. **Fonts**: change main font used in presentation
    c. **Effects**: adjust the appearance of objects e.g., shadow, border, etc.
    d. **Background Styles**: Select fill color, gradient, or picture
    e. **Hide Background Graphics**: used to hide background pictures
3. Click **Close Master View**

Changing master slide background color palette

1.1.2 Modify slide master content

Modifying content in the slide master view will update all slides, maintaining a consistent layout.

Modify master slide content:

1. While in Slide Master view, select the master slide (first slide on left)
2. Select text or objects, and modify as follows:
   a. **Delete**: press delete key
   b. **Move**: drag with mouse or tap/press arrow keys
   c. **Rotate**: drag rotation icon, hold shift to snap to common angles
   d. **Resize**: drag corner/edge grips, affects text wrapping when present
   e. **Format Shape**: right-click and select Format Shape for additional options

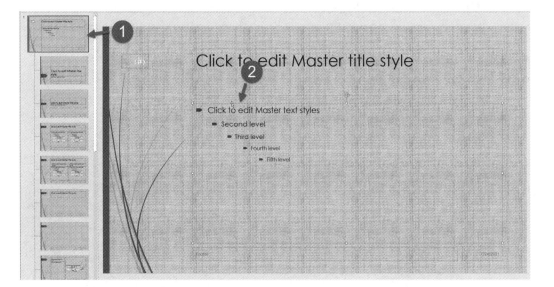

Modifying master slide content

1.1.3 Create slide layouts

New slide layouts may be created to organize specific of content in a consistent manner.

Create a new slide layout:

1. While in Slide Master view, click **Insert Layout**
2. **Right-click** on the new layout
3. Select **Rename Layout**
4. **Type** a new name and click **OK**
5. Insert and modify **placeholder content**

Use the **Slide Master → Insert Placeholder** to define the location for text, pictures, chats, and more. Modify the content on the new layout per the steps previously covered.

Creating a new slide layout

1.1.4 Modify slide layouts

Modifying content in the slide master view will update all slides, maintaining a consistent layout.

Modify master slide content:

1. While in Slide Master view, select a master slide **Layout**
2. Select text or objects, and modify as follows:
    a. **Delete**: press delete key
    b. **Move**: drag with mouse or tap/press arrow keys
    c. **Rotate**: drag rotation icon, hold shift to snap to common angles
    d. **Resize**: drag corner/edge grips, affects text wrapping when present
    e. **Format Shape**: right-click and select Format Shape for additional options

Modifying slide layouts

In addition to modifying content, it is also possible to add new content. Select **Slide Master\Insert Placeholder** and select from the options.

1.1.5 Modify the handout master

The handout master organizes one or more slides onto a single page with header and footer information, such as date and page number. The layout of this handout may be modified.

Modify handout master: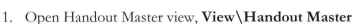

1. Open Handout Master view, **View\Handout Master**
2. Select options on **Handout Master** tab, such as:
    a. **Page Setup**: Orientation, Size, and Slides per Page
    b. **Placeholders**: Header, Footer, Date, Page Number
    c. **Background**: Colors, Fonts, Effects, Styles, Hide

Modifying the handout master

Notice, the **Slides per Page** options shown in the image above correspond to the options shown to the right, when printing.

Related print options

1.1.6 Modify the notes master

The notes master organizes talking points for each slide. When printing, it is possible to select Notes Pages as the Print Layout. In this case the notes master layout is used. This layout may be modified.

Modify notes master:

1. Open Notes Master view, **View\Notes Master**
2. Select options on **Notes Master** tab, such as (see image on next page):
   a. **Page Setup**: Orientation, Size
   b. **Placeholders**: Header, Image, Footer, Date, Body, Page Number
   c. **Theme**: Select an option
   d. **Background**: Colors, Fonts, Effects, Styles, Hide

The Notes Master layout will be used when Notes Pages is selected as shown in the image to the right.

Related print option

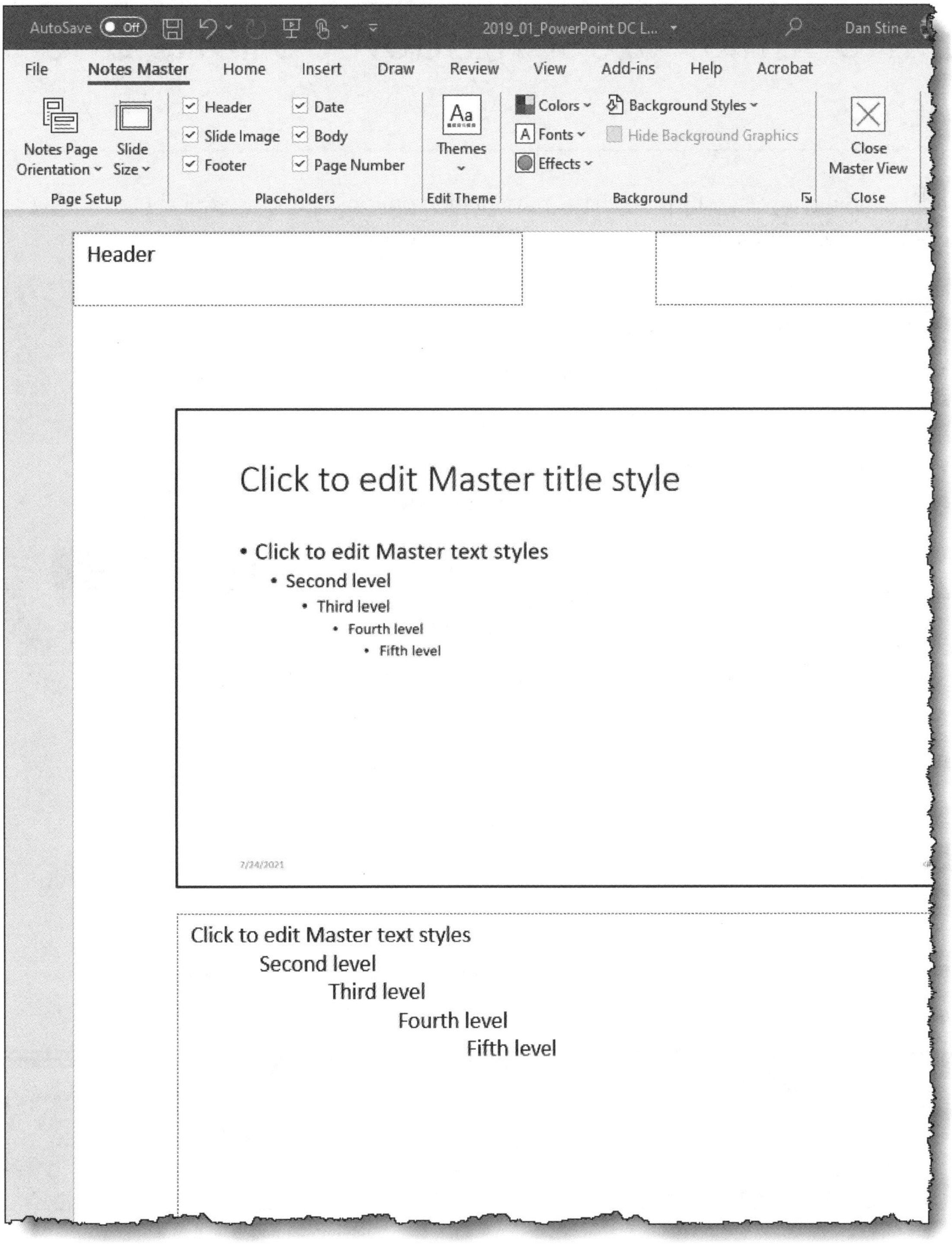

Modifying the notes master

1.2 Change presentation options and views

Understanding how to control the basic presentation options and views will aid in creating clear and concise presentations in a very efficient manner.

1.2.0 Basic slide deck navigation

There are several ways in which one can navigate a slide deck within PowerPoint. This section covers a few of the most popular.

Use arrow keys to change the current slide

Using the arrow keys steps through the current slide deck.

1. Click within a slide (to make it active)
2. Use to arrows on the keyboard as follows:
    a. Down arrow – advance to next slide (or Right key)
    b. Up arrow – move back to the previous slide (or Left key)

Select a preview slide

Selecting a slide preview quickly jumps to that slide, making it active for editing.

1. Click on a preview slide, on the left, to make that slide current

Zoom within a slide

1. To zoom within a slide, do one of the following:
    a. Drag the zoom slider in the lower left corner of the PowerPoint window
    b. While holding the Ctrl key, spin the wheel on the mouse

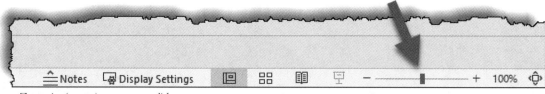

Zoom in (or out) on current slide

1.2.1 Change slide size

The size of the slides within a PowerPoint document may be changed. The default size is set to Widescreen, which matches most monitors and projection screens. However, for an ultra-wide display or a conference room display panel, the slide size may need to be modified.

Modify slide size

1. Click the **Design** tab on the Ribbon
2. Select **Slide Size → Custom Slide Size…**
3. To change the size, either:
   a. Select from the **Slides sized for list**, or
   b. Select **Custom** and enter a Width and Height

Slide Size dialog

4. Select a content scaling options (if prompted):
   a. **Maximize**: content is scaled and stretched to fit new size
   b. **Ensure Fit**: content is only scaled to maintain original proportions

Slide size change scaling options

1.2.2 Display presentations in different views

When working on a presentation, on your computer, there are different ways to view the content, depending on your current task.

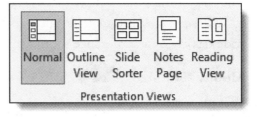

In addition to Presenter mode, covered later in this chapter, there are five ways to view the content in the current file. Simply toggle between them on the View tab.

Here is what each view mode is for:

A. **Normal**
   Default option, with large editable view of current slide and thumbnail view of all slides on left. This is the mode used most often when developing a presentation.

B. **Outline View**
   Large editable view of current slide with full presentation outline on left. This view is also an option when printing.

C. **Slide Sorter**
   Non-editable view of all slides, grouped by sections if they exist. This mode is used to manually rearrange slides (via drag and drop) within the slide deck.

D. **Notes Page**
   Single page view, with one slide and notes associated with that slide. This view is also an option when printing.

E. **Reading View**
   Similar to presentation mode, a single slide fills the application window, but not the entire screen. Use this mode to review a presentation without filling a second screen (like in presentation mode) if you have one. Press **Esc** to exit Reading View.

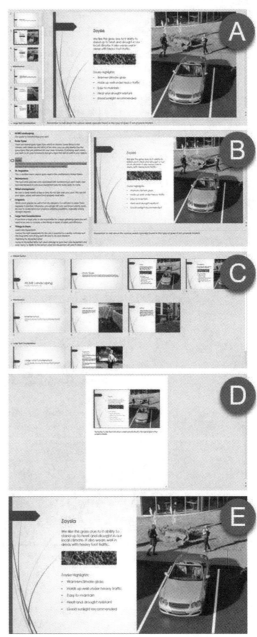

Display options compared

1.2.3 Set basic file properties

Each PowerPoint document has a place to enter unique properties used to track and identify it. These properties are also referred to as metadata and may be viewed without opening the file.

Modify document properties

1. Click the **File** tab on the Ribbon
2. Select **Info**
3. Select the **Properties** drop-down list and click **Advanced Properties**
4. Modify the document properties in the open dialog

When finished, to save the changes and return to the document, click the OK button and then the left-pointing arrow (in a circle) in the upper left.

Document properties

This information can be made visible via Window's **file explorer** as shown here for "Authors".

Column added to windows explorer to show author info from files listed

1.3 Configure print settings for presentations

This section will cover several print settings one needs to be familiar with when taking the certification exam.

1.3.0 The all-digital presentation

Before looking at the various print setting, note that there are several options to create, deliver, and leave-behind all digital content. However, even in this case, the print settings found in this section are important, as they directly impact the quality and legibility of your digital content.

There are several reasons to maintain an all-digital presentation, as opposed to printer boards, notes, and handouts for the audience. The two big ones are:

- **Content is always current**
  Printed content can become outdated the moment it is printed. An all-digital presentation can be modified seconds before a presentation.

- **Sustainability**
  Not printing, when practical, saves on resources (e.g. printing, paper, power) and helps protect the environment.

Digital Notes
Notes can be viewed on-screen when there are two monitors, while in presentation mode. The "two screens" can be a laptop display (showing notes) and a projector/display (showing presentation). Notes could also be loaded, manually, onto a tablet you hold, allowing you to walk about while presenting.

Digital handouts
PowerPoint presentations can also be used as a handout or leave-behind for the audience. PowerPoint can export PDF and PowerPoint Presentation (*.pptx) files which may be emailed or electronically shared in various ways.

Digital presentations
The main presentation can be shared digitally in many ways, including via video conference, digital projector, flat screen display, or recorded video.

1.3.1 Print all or part of a presentation

When printing a presentation, either to hardcopy or PDF, it is possible to control the portion of presentation to be printed.

Print range selection

1. Click the **File** tab on the Ribbon
2. Select **Print**
3. Print Range options (default is all slides):
   a. Enter **Slides** to print, e.g. 1-6, or 1-4, 6, 10-12
   b. Select from drop-down list:
      - Current slide only
      - Specific section
      - Print selection (selected before entering print settings)

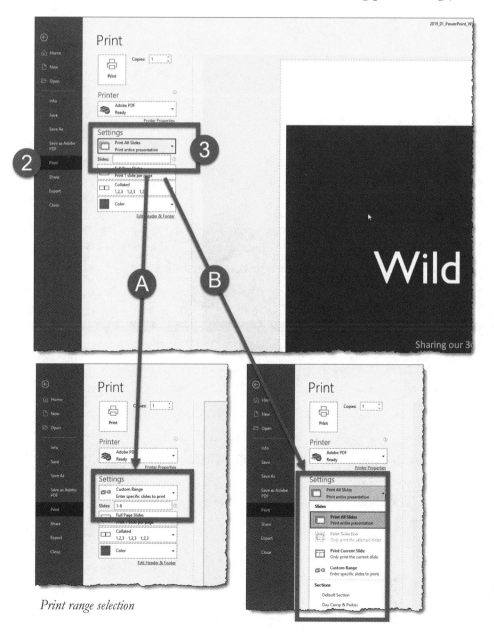

Print range selection

1.3.2 Print notes pages

When printing, it is possible to print your notes, alongside each slide. Here's how…

Print notes pages

1. Click the **File** tab on the Ribbon
2. Select **Print**
3. Select **Notes Pages**
   - Image to right shows drop-down menu options
4. Preview printed results

Print layout options

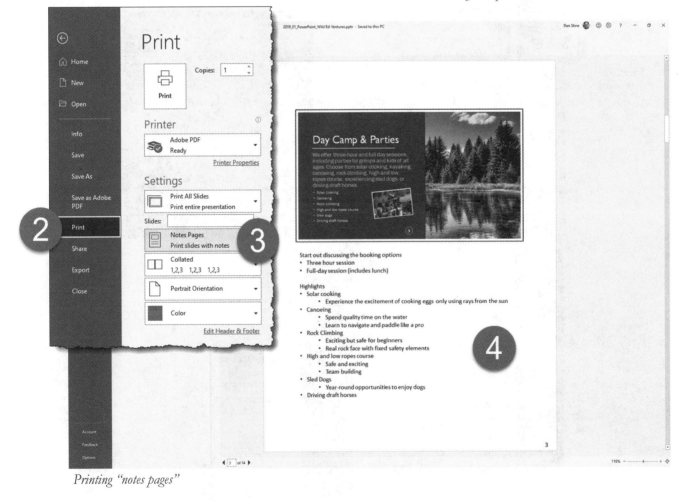

Printing "notes pages"

1.3.3 Print handouts

When printing, there is an option to print multiple slides per page.

Print handouts

1. Click the **File** tab on the Ribbon
2. Select **Print**
3. Click the drop-down list shown
4. Select a **Handouts** option
5. Preview printed results

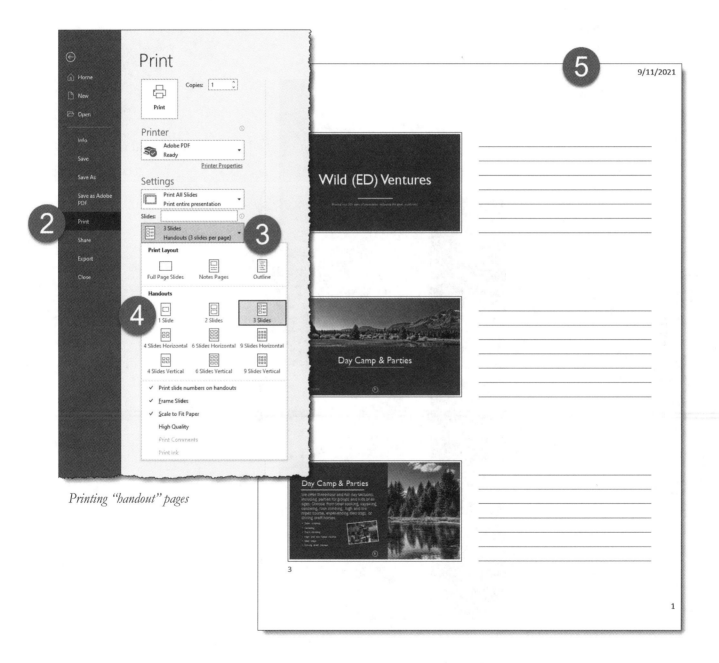

Printing "handout" pages

1.3.4 Print in color, grayscale, or black and white

When printing, there is an option to print in color, black and white, or grayscale. The default is color, and what is used most often. When a color document is printed on a non-color printer, it will be grayscale automatically. However, printing black and white or grayscale is preferred at times, for example, to avoid implied color selection or to verify the grayscale tones are legible (note, a darker color like green will be a darker gray than a lighter color like yellow).

Print color options

1. Click the **File** tab on the Ribbon
2. Select **Print**
3. Select a color option
    a. Color (default)
    b. Grayscale
    c. Pure Black and White

The last option, Pure Black and White, is used sparingly as it can make some images and text difficult or impossible to understand.

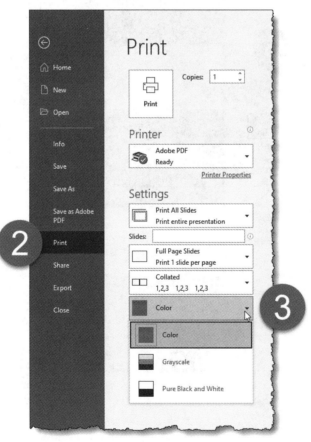

Print color options

1.4 Configure and present slide shows

Once a PowerPoint slide deck has been developed, it is helpful to know the various ways in which the software can aid in delivering the presentation to an audience.

1.4.0 Spelling and grammar corrections
A final recommended step, before presenting or publishing a PowerPoint slide deck, is to perform a spelling and grammar check.

Spell and Grammer corrections

1. **Spelling:** Right-click on red underlined text
2. Options
    a. Select a correct spelling option
    b. Select **Ignore All**: helpful for product names not in the dictionary
    c. Select **Add to Dictionary**: helpful if it is your product name
3. **Grammar:** Right-click on blue underlined text
    a. Consider the suggestion
    b. In this example, the problem is partly caused by a missing word

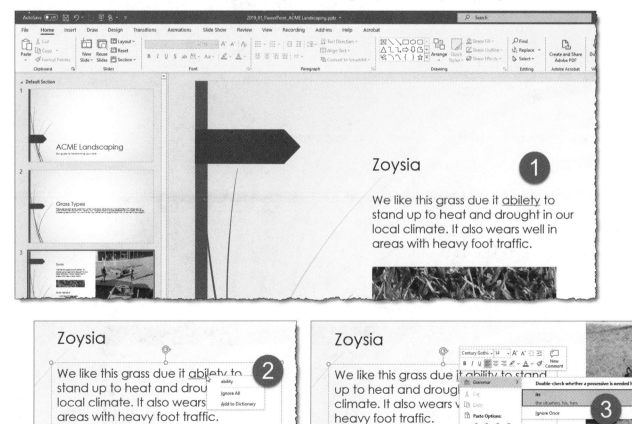

Spelling and grammar corrections

1.4.1 Create custom slide shows

Presentations can be customized into smaller sub-sets of the overall slide deck. For example, a comprehensive presentation on landscaping services can be paired down to just maintenance services, which looks more professional, as you are not having to skip slides.

Create a custom slide show

1. Click **Slide Show** (tab) →
   Custom Slide Show →
   Custom Shows…
2. Select **New…**
3. Define the slide show
   a. Provide a name
   b. Select slides to include
   c. Click **Add** button
   d. Rearrange included slide order, or remove slides
   e. Click **OK** to finish
4. Click **Close**
5. Notice new option under **Custom Slide Shows**

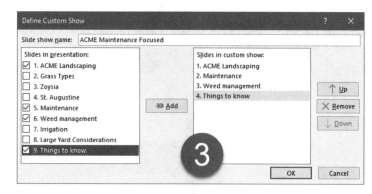

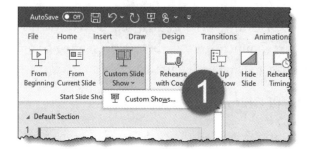

Clicking the custom slide show option starts presentation mode, based only on the selected slides. The other slides are not accessible until the presentation mode is ended (by pressing Esc).

Using this technique allows a comprehensive presentation to be used in multiple ways, without needing to make copies of the file and risk data getting out of sync between them.

Creating a custom slide show

1.4.2 Configure slide show options

There are several presenter settings which can be adjusted before the presentation begins. These settings can help make things go more smoothly while getting ready to present.

Revit ribbon Set Up options

1. Click **Slide Show** (tab) on the ribbon
2. Review/adjust the options in the **Set Up** panel

Slide show "set up" options on the Ribbon

Set Up Slide Show

1. Click **Slide Show** (tab) → **Set Up Slide Show**
2. Review/adjust the options as needed
3. Click **OK** to finish

Set Up Slide Show options dialog

The options are mostly self-explanatory. Click the "**?**" in the upper right of the dialog box for Help. See the remaining topics in this section for additional related information.

1.4.3 Rehearse slide show timing

There are several presenter settings which can be adjusted before the presentation begins. These settings can help make things go more smoothly while getting ready to present.

Rehearse timings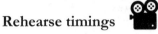

1. Click **Slide Show** (tab) → **Rehearse Timings** on the ribbon
2. Rehearse timings as follows:
   a. Practice talking about the current slide
   b. Advance slide (arrow in Recording toolbar, click, down/right arrow)
   c. First number is time on current slide, second is total time
   d. Exit rehearse timings mode: **Esc** or click the "x" in the Recording toolbar
3. Save timings options:
   a. **Yes**: sets slides to auto advance using rehearsed timings
   b. **No**: does not modify slide transition settings
   c. Notice the total slide show time is listed here

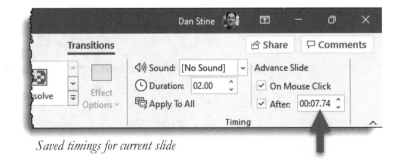

Rehearse slide show timings

If slide timings are saved, the results may be seen on the Transitions tab as shown in the image below. The default "After" is not checked and the Advance Slide timing is set to 00:00.00. Note that once changed, like the example below, anytime a Presentation is started, these timings will be used and the slide will automatically advance.

Saved timings for current slide

1.4.4 Set up slide show recording options

Before recording a slide show, there are a few settings to be aware of to help ensure a successful and high-quality recording.

The options in the **Slide Show** ➔ **Set Up** panel also apply to recordings.

Slide show recording options on the ribbon

Slide show recording options

1. Click **Slide Show** (tab) ➔ **Record Slide Show** on the ribbon
2. Adjust the following options, as needed:
    a. **Clear**, Clear recordings for Current or all slides
    b. **Settings**, Select microphone/camera if more than one option exists
    c. **Toggles**
        • **Microphone**: mute or unmute
        • **Camera**: on or off
        • **Camera preview**: show or hide

Slide show recording options while in presentation mode

1.4.5 Present slide shows by using Presenter View

On a computer with multiple monitors, Presenter View can be used. This view offers an expanded view and control of the presentation, not seen by the audience.

Use Presnter View

1. From the **Slide Show** tab, select **From Beginning** or **From Current Slide**
2. Use the Presenter View as follows:
   a. **Show Taskbar**, use if other Windows apps need to be accessed
   b. **Display Settings**:
      - Swap Presenter View to the other screen
      - Duplicate, show full presentation on both screens
   c. End Slide Show, exit the presentation
   d. Presentation options:
      - Draw, view all slides, zoom, blank display, subtitles, menu
   e. Note for current slide (if any exist)
      - Adjust text size with icons in lower left
   f. Navigate slides, forwards or backwards
      - Current slide shown above
      - Next slide shown on right

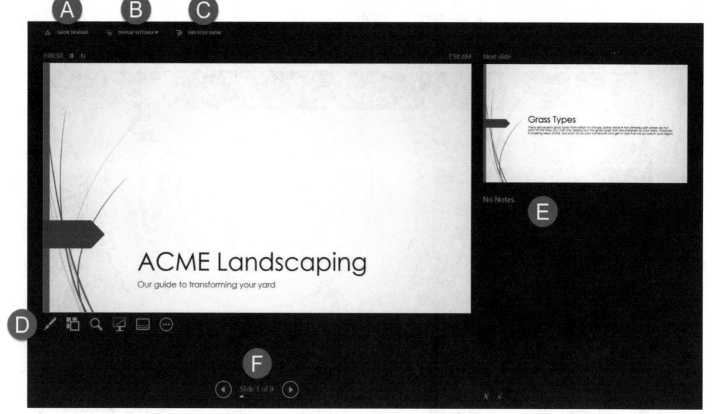

Overview of presenter view

1.5 Prepare presentations for collaboration

In our highly connected world, it is important to know how to collaborate and share content with others.

1.5.0 Save and close a presentation

Know how to properly save and close PowerPoint to preserve the integrity of your data.

Save and Close a presentation

1. From the **File** tab, select; **Save**
    a. Provide name and location of file for first save
2. Select **Close**, to exit the PowerPoint application
    a. You will be prompted to save, for any unsaved files that are open

Saving and closing a presentation

1.5.1 Mark presentations as final

When a presentation is finished it can be helpful for future reference and to let other presenters know it is finished by marking it as final.

Mark as final

1. Click the **File** tab
2. Select the **Info** tab on the left
3. Click the **Protect Presentation** drop-down
4. Select **Mark as Final**
5. Click **OK** to prompt, which will save the document
6. Click **OK** to information about "mark as final"

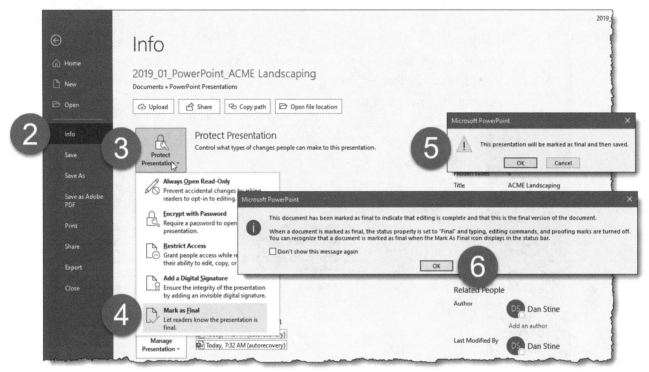

Marking a presentation as final to avoid accidental changes

When the presentation is opened in the future, a message is displayed at the top, and the Ribbon tools are hidden to prevent accidental changes. If changes are required, simply click the **Edit Anyway** button.

Marked as Final message when document first opened

1.5.2 Protect presentations by using passwords

When a document contains confidential information, it can be protected by requiring a password to open it. This is especially helpful if presenting on a shared/public computer.

Protect presentation with password

1. Click the **File** tab
2. Select the **Info** tab on the left
3. Click the **Protect Presentation** drop-down
4. Select **Encrypt with Password**
5. Enter a password and click **OK**   **Tip:** Read the caution note shown
6. Re-enter the same password and click **OK**

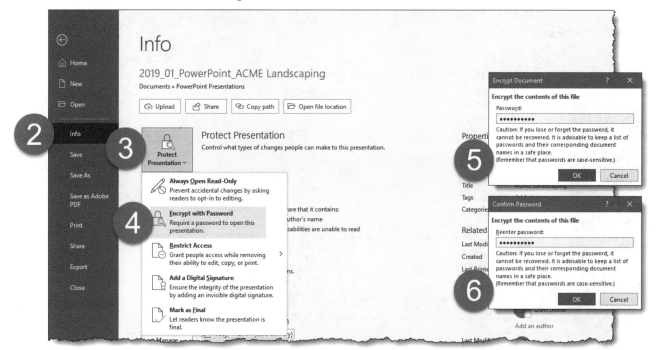

Protecting a presentation with a password

In the future, when a protected presentation is opened, a password will be required (similar to the example shown below). Note that passwords are **case sensitive**. If the password is lost, the file cannot be opened; and Microsoft will not help with this problem. **A password can be removed**, once the document has been opened, by following the above and erasing the password when prompted to provide one.

Password prompt when opening a presentation

1.5.3 Inspect presentations for issues

Before sharing/collaborating with a document, check it for issues – such as personal information or comments.

Inspect document for issues

1. Click the **File** tab
2. Select the **Info** tab on the left
3. Click the **Check for Issues** drop-down
4. Select **Inspect Document**
5. Document Inspector dialog:
   a. Select document sections to check (all are checked by default)
   b. Click the **Inspect** button
6. Review and/or resolve issues
   a. Note issues discovered
   b. Click the **Remove All** button, as needed, for each section

Inspecting presentation for issues

1.5.4 Add and manage comments

Comments are used to track feedback and required changes to the presentation.

Add comments

1. On the **Review** tab, click the **New Comment** button
2. In the **Comments** pane, enter a comment and press **Enter** to finish
3. Notice the comment icon in the upper left, which signifies a comment on this slide
4. Toggle the Comments pane on and off with the **Show Comments** command

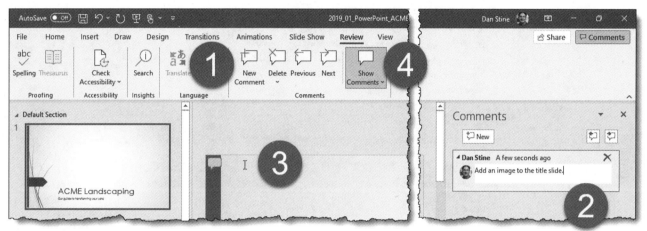

Adding comments to the current presentation/slide

Manage comments

Comments can be managed within the Comments pane. Toggle this on and off using the Show Comments option on the Review tab. As shown in the image below, comments can be replied to (click in Reply… area and start typing) or deleted (click the "X" in the upper right).

Managing a previously created comment

1.5.5 Preserve presentation content

When sharing a presentation, custom fonts can be embedded and media can be compressed.

Preserve fidelity by embedding fonts

1. On the **File** tab, click the **Options** command
2. Select the **Save** tab, and check to **Embed fonts**

PowerPoint Options	? ✕

General
Proofing
Save
Language
Ease of Access
Advanced
Customize Ribbon
Quick Access Toolbar
Add-ins
Trust Center

☑ AutoSave OneDrive and SharePoint Online files by default on PowerPoint ⓘ

Save files in this format: `PowerPoint Presentation`

☑ Save AutoRecover information every `10` minutes
  ☑ Keep the last AutoRecovered version if I close without saving

AutoRecover file location: `C:\Users\Dan Stine\AppData\Roaming\Microsoft\PowerPoint\`

☐ Don't show the Backstage when opening or saving files with keyboard shortcuts

☑ Show additional places for saving, even if sign-in may be required.

☐ Save to Computer by default

Default local file location: `C:\Users\Dan Stine\Documents\`

Default personal templates location: `C:\Users\Dan Stine\Documents\Custom Office Templates\`

Offline editing options for document management server files

Saving checked out files to server drafts is no longer supported. Checked out files are now saved to the Office Document Cache.

Learn more

Server drafts location: `C:\Users\Dan Stine\Documents\SharePoint Drafts\`

Preserve fidelity when sharing this presentation: `2019_01_PowerPoint_ACME Landscaping.pptx`

☑ Embed fonts in the file ⓘ
  ● Embed only the characters used in the presentation (best for reducing file size)
  ○ Embed all characters (best for editing by other people)

Cache Settings

Days to keep files in the Office Document Cache: `14`

☐ Delete files from the Office Document Cache when they are closed

Delete files in the cache that have been saved for faster viewing. This will not delete items pending upload to the server, nor items with upload errors. | Delete cached files |

| OK | Cancel |

Preserving presentation fidelity

Compress media content (when present)

1. On the **File** tab, click the **Info** tab
2. **Optimize** or **Compress** media (available only if file contains media content)
3. Select from options and follow prompts

Compressing/optimizing media content

1.5.6 Export presentations to other formats

A presentation can be exported to other formats, such as a PDF, to be shared with others who may not have PowerPoint on their computer, or do not need to present the information.

Export presentation to other formats

1. Select the **File** tab
2. Select the **Export** tab
3. Select an export format option
   a. Click **Change File Type** for more options
4. Click the **Create** option
5. Provide a file name and location to save the new file
   a. Some add-ins, like Adobe Acrobat, provide additional options

Exporting the current presentation as another format

Some add-ins provide additional options

1.6 Practice tasks

Try the topics covered in this chapter to make sure you understand the concepts. These tasks are sequential and should be completed in the same PowerPoint document unless noted otherwise. Saving the results is optional, unless assigned by an instructor.

First Step:

✓ Open provided document **Danish Potato Salad Recipe.pptx**

Task 1.1:

✓ Create a new Master Slide **Layout** named **Table Ready Photos**.

Task 1.2

✓ Change the slide size to **Standard (4:3)** using the Ensure Fit option.

Task 1.3

✓ Create a custom slide show, called **Quick Demo**, containing only slides 2 and 4.

Task 1.4:

✓ Use **Inspect Document** to find and remove **Comments**.

Task 1.5:

✓ Mark the presentation as final then save and close.

1.7 Self-exam & review questions

Self-Exam:

The following questions can be used to check your knowledge of this chapter. The answers can be found at the bottom of the next page.

1. PowerPoint documents are commonly started from templates. (T/F)
2. The file extension for a PowerPoint document is .pptx. (T/F)
3. The slide master controls the content on each slide. (T/F)
4. Which ribbon tab is Mark as Final found on? _____.
5. Microsoft will help recover lost document passwords. (T/F)

Review Questions:

The following questions may be assigned by your instructor to assess your knowledge of this chapter. Your instructor has the answers to the review questions.

1. When rehearsing slide show timings, the first number is time spent on current slide, and the second is total time. (T/F)
2. Check for Issues does not look for comments. (T/F)
3. The presentation Theme can be changed while editing the slide master. (T/F)
4. The Show Comments command is found on the View tab. (T/F)
5. Custom slide shows are used to rearrange and omit slides in a presentation. (T/F)
6. A printed "notes page" contains one slide and notes for that slide. (T/F)
7. Where are the document properties found? _____ .
8. Presentations may be printed in color or grayscale, but not black and white. (T/F)
9. The default view, for a presentation, is Normal. (T/F)
10. Modifying content in the slide master view will update all slides. (T/F)

Notes:

2 Manage Slides

Introduction

This chapter covers the ways in which a PowerPoint slide deck can be managed to organize, control visibility of slides and footers/headers/page numbers, and more.

2.0 Slide thumbnails

In addition to the thumbnail views found in Slide Sorter view, covered in the previous chapter, the thumbnail views shown in Normal view have several functions.

2.0.0 Presentation views - Normal

The thumbnail views presented on the left, while in Normal view, offer a number of functions. For example, the width may be adjusted, making the thumbnails larger or smaller. Additionally, right-clicking on a slide, or between two, offers several functions, such as Duplicate slide, Delete slide, Insert Slide, etc. Finally, slides may be rearranged as follows…

Rearrange slides in Normal view:

1. Click and drag on a slide
2. Drop the slide in its new location

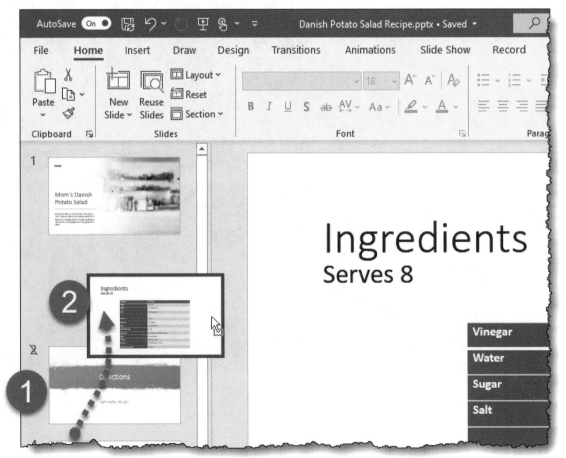

Repositioning slides via thumbnail sidebar

2.1 Insert slides

Understanding how to work with slides and slide content is important in the process of efficiently creating a highly effective presentation.

2.1.0 Extracting slide content

An often-overlooked opportunity to quickly access content within a presentation is the process of renaming the .pptx file to .zip in Windows Explorer. Doing so provides unique access to content, such as media (images and videos). The first image below shows the renamed file, while the second shows the contents of the newly renamed file. In this example, the images and video files may be copy/pasted to another folder for use in other applications.

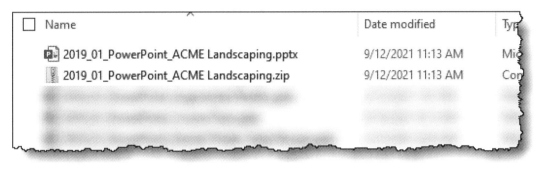

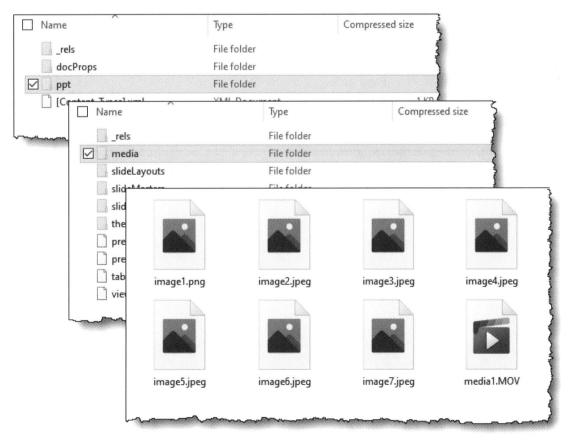

2.1.1 Import Word document outlines

It is possible to start a presentation outline using Microsoft Word and then import it into PowerPoint in such a way that several slides are created based on formatting.

Rearrange slides in Normal view:

1. Create an outline in Word; see formatting requirements on next page
    a. FYI: Style setting shown for reference below, and not actually in Word doc.
2. In PowerPoint, select Insert → New Slide (drop-down)
3. Click Slides from Outline…
4. Browse to Word document, click Insert, and review results

ACME Landscaping (Title)

Grass Types (Heading 1)

Zoysia (Heading 1)
We like this grass due to its ability to stand up to heat and drought in our local climate. It also wears well in areas with heavy foot traffic. (Normal)

- Zoysia Highlights (Heading 2)
    o Warmer-climate grass (Heading 3)
    o Holds up well under heavy traffic (Heading 3)
    o Add more points (Heading 3)

St. Augustine (Heading 1)
This is another warm season grass used in the southeastern United States. (Normal)

- St. Augustine Highlights (Heading 2)
    o Dense and full look (Heading 3)
    o Crowds out weeds (Heading 3)
    o Add more points (Heading 3)

Maintenance (Heading 1)
After all the hard work and real costs put into transforming your yard, it needs care and maintenance to ensure your investment lasts for many years to come. (Normal)

Weed management (Heading 1)
    o List points here (Heading 2)

Irrigation (Heading 1)
    o List points here (Heading 2)

Large Yard Considerations (Heading 1)

Things to know (Heading 1)
    o List points here (Heading 2)

Word document with title and heading styles applied

Word document formatting

When inserting a Word document outline PowerPoint will only use text set to the following styles:

- Title
- Heading 1, 2, 3, etc.

Title and Heading 1 styles become separate slides. Headings 2 and higher become bulleted items. Everything else, normal text and images, are ignored. Compare the Word outline shown on the previous page with the resultant PowerPoint slides created in the image below.

Change Slide Layout

Right-click on a slide thumbnail and change the slide Layout as needed to prepare each slide for required content.

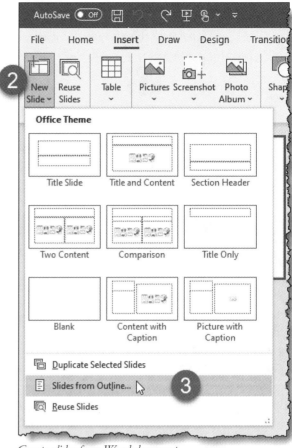

Create slides from Word document

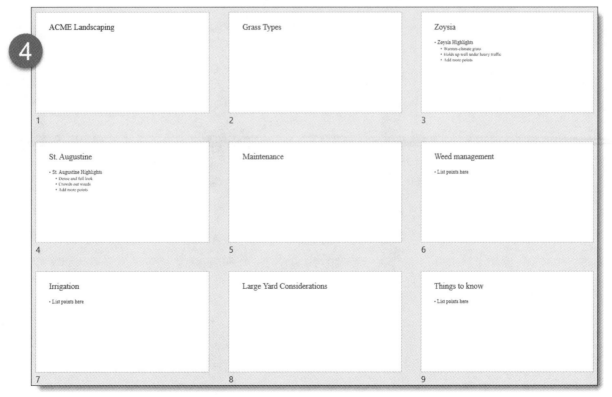

Resultant slides created in PowerPoint from Word document

2.1.2 Insert slides from another presentation

Without opening other PowerPoint presentation files directly, it is possible to insert slides from them. Slides are inserted, not linked, immediately after the current slide.

Reuse Slides:

1. Select **Reuse Slides** from the Home or Insert tab
2. Click **Browse** in the Reuse Slides pane, select a PowerPoint file
3. Click **Insert Slide** for desired slides
4. Review results, reposition within slide deck as required

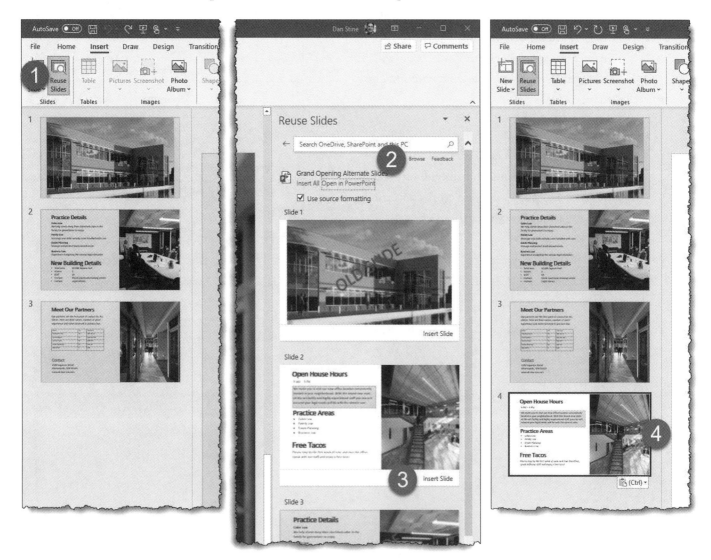

Inserting a slide from another presentation file

2.1.3 Insert slides and select slide layouts

When creating a new slide, it is possible to specify the Layout, saving time adding and organizing content on them.

Insert slide with specific layout:

1. Select **New Slide** (drop-down) from the Home or Insert tab
2. Select a **Layout** option
    - Title Slide
    - Title and Content
    - Section Header
    - Etc.

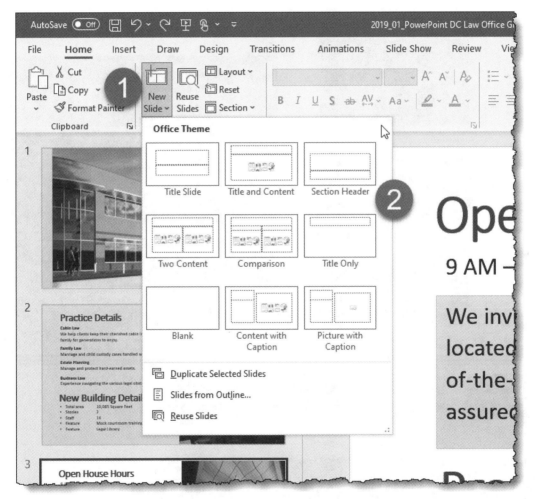

Insert a slide with a specified layout

To change a layout later, after a new slide has been created, simply right-click on a slide thumbnail and change the slide Layout as needed.

2.1.4 Insert Summary Zoom slides

Using a Summary Zoom slide is an interactive, non-linear way to navigate a slide deck during a presentation. The slide is placed right after the title slide. Clicking on a thumbnail will jump to that slide/section. After the slide/section, you are automatically returned to the summary zoom slide to pick your next option, which may have changed based on audience feedback from the previous slide/section.

Insert Summary Zoom slides:

1. Select **Zoom (drop-down)** → **Summary Zoom** from the Insert tab
2. Select the slides or sections and then click the Insert button
3. Observe the results

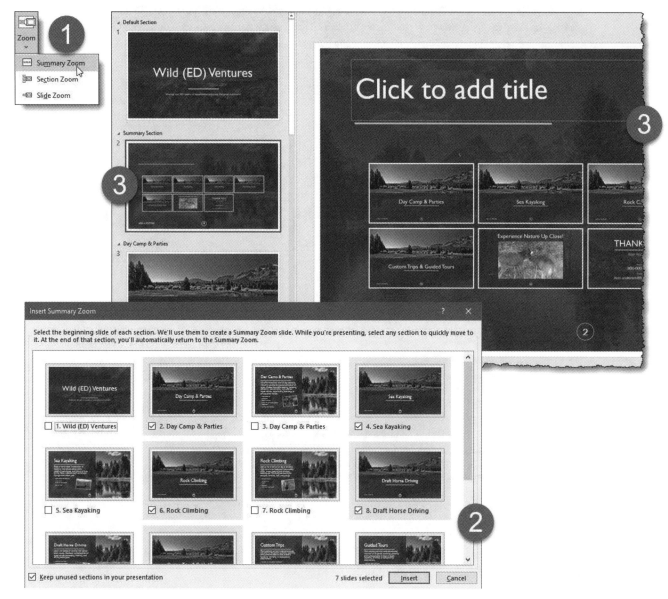

Inserting a summary zoom slide

2.1.5 Duplicate slides

Sometimes it is more efficient to duplicate a slide and modify its contents rather than start a new slide from scratch.

Duplicate a slide:

1. **Right-click** on a slide thumbnail in the side bar
2. Select **Duplicate slide**
3. Observe the results

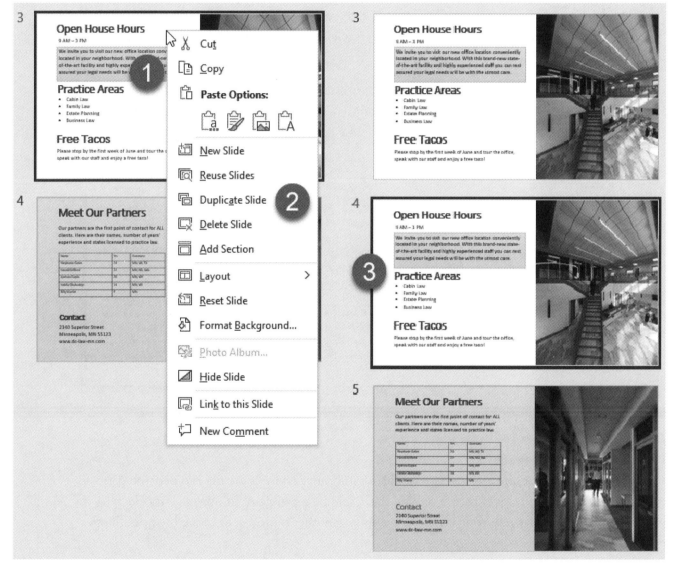

Duplicating a slide

2.2 Modify slides

It is important to know how to make simple modifications to the slides in a presentation. This will help convey the information to your audience in the best way possible. It will also help if changes have been made by others, like hiding a slide, which is now needed to appear in a presentation.

2.2.0 Presentation file size

As a presentation continues to develop and slides are modified, the size of the PowerPoint file (.pptx) will increase. It is helpful to keep track of the file size and understand when file size matters.

The file size can be seen within PowerPoint, from the **File tab → Info** area. It can also be observed from Windows **File Explorer** (aka My Computer) as shown below. From File Explorer, the presentation files may be sorted by name, date, size by clicking on the header text.

Name	Date modified	Type	Size	Authors
2019_01_PowerPoint DC Law Office Grand Opening.pptx	2/13/2021 8:53 AM	Microsoft PowerP...	543 KB	Dan Stine
2019_01_PowerPoint_ACME Landscaping.pptx	9/12/2021 11:13 AM	Microsoft PowerP...	16,420 KB	Dan Stine
2019_01_PowerPoint_ACME Landscaping.zip	9/12/2021 11:13 AM	Compressed (zipp...	16,420 KB	
2019_01_PowerPoint_Augmented Reality.pptx	2/13/2021 7:01 PM	Microsoft PowerP...	937 KB	Dan Stine
2019_01_PowerPoint_Course Flyer.pptx	9/19/2021 9:13 AM	Microsoft PowerP...	42 KB	Dan Stine
2019_01_PowerPoint_Danish Potato Salad Recipe.pptx	2/15/2021 8:24 AM	Microsoft PowerP...	707 KB	Dan Stine
2019_01_PowerPoint_Imagine This.pptx	2/14/2021 11:41 AM	Microsoft PowerP...	594 KB	Dan Stine
2019_01_PowerPoint_Wild Ed-Ventures.pptx	9/11/2021 9:58 AM	Microsoft PowerP...	4,980 KB	Dan Stine
August 2021 Fall Semester Presentation - Copy.pptx	6/20/2021 9:24 AM	Microsoft PowerP...	0 KB	
Grand Opening Alternate Slides.pptx	2/13/2021 8:55 AM	Microsoft PowerP...	657 KB	Dan Stine
January 2022 Spring Semester Presentation.pptx	6/20/2021 9:24 AM	Microsoft PowerP...	0 KB	

The file size may not matter with a couple of common exceptions.

Low hard disk space

When a presentation contains a lot of videos and other content the file can become very large. If your hard drive space is limited this could be a problem. In this case, try cleaning up your hard drive by removing old files and apps. Another option is to move the pptx file to the cloud.

Sending presentation via email

Before sending a pptx file as an attachment to an email, double check its file size. In general, try to avoid sending files over 2 MB – notice three of the files above are too large to email. In this case, consider sending a download link via OneDrive, Dropbox, etc.

2.2.1 Hide and unhide slides

Occasionally, a slide may not be complete or will become irrelevant and need to be hidden. If there is a chance you may be needed again, the best option is to hide the slide rather than delete it.

Hide a slide: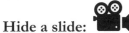

When a slide is hidden, it is still seen in the slide deck, but does not show up in presentation mode.

1. **Right-click** on a slide thumbnail in the side bar
2. Select **Hide slide** *to toggle it hidden*
3. Observe slide number has a slash through it

Unhide a slide:

1. **Right-click** on a slide thumbnail in the side bar
2. Select **Hide slide** *to toggle it unhidden*
3. Observe slide number no longer has a slash through it

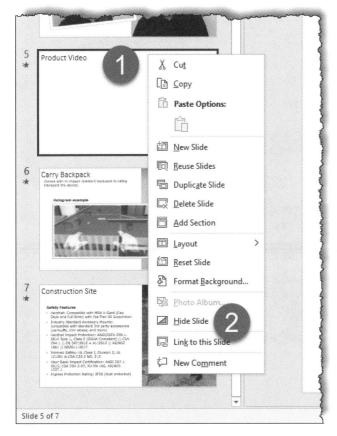
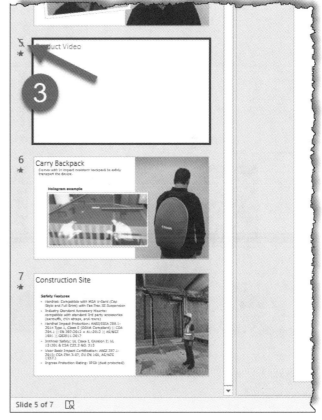

Hiding a slide (same steps to unhide)

2.2.2 Modify individual slide backgrounds

Each slide can have its background modified as covered here.

Format Slide Background: 🎥

1. **Select** a slide to make it current
2. Click **Format Background** from the Design tab
3. Modify the background projects as needed
   a. E.g. select Gradient Fill and adjust the color and gradient sliders
4. Observe the results for the current slide

Modify a slide's background

2.2.3 Insert slide headers, footers, and page numbers

Slides may have footer information such as date/time, slide number, and custom text to indicate the document is confidential or a draft, for example. Technically, a presentation slide does not have a header option, other than manually adding a textbox at the top of the slide in a slide master/layout view.

Add Footer and page numbers:

1. From the Insert tab, select **Header & Footer**, **Slide Number**, or **Date & Time**
   a. FYI: All three commands open the same dialog shown in the next step
2. Make the desired adjustments in the **Header and Footer dialog**, then:
   a. **Apply** – applies changes to current slide only
   b. **Apply to All** – applies changes to all slides in the presentation
3. Observe the results

Managing slide footer

2.3 Order and group slides

This last section covers ways in which slides within your presentation can be organized and rearranged as the project develops or needs to change over time.

2.3.0 Introduction

A well-organized slide can not only help the individuals who created the presentation, but others who were not involved in the creation of the slide deck but need to present it to others. This can happen as a company grows or a large sales team need to use a company provided presentation to pitch a specific product to an audience.

In the example presentation below, notice the slides are grouped into sections, on the left, and some sections have been collapsed to better visualize the slide deck at a high level. The current slide, on the right, also has clear notes at the bottom to help the presenter recall all the important points to make while presenting.

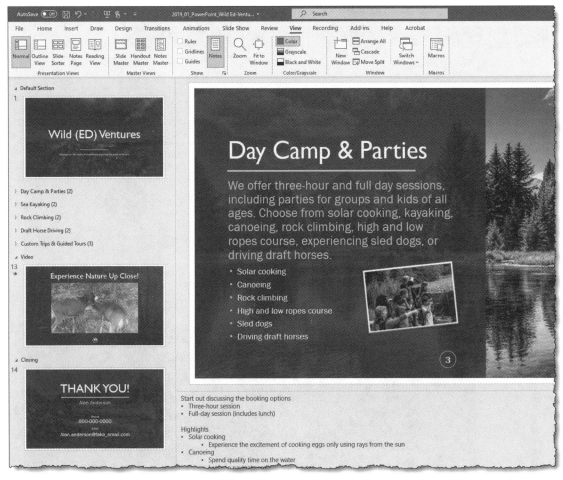

Example of a well-organized presentation

2.3.1 Create sections

Larger presentations, with many slides, benefit from sections. Sections are used to group presentation topics, and can also hide slide, in the sidebar on the left, when not needed.

Create sections:

1. Select first slide to be included in section
2. Pick Home → Section → Add Section
3. Enter a Section name
4. Review results

Clicking on the small arrow icon to the left of the section name will collapse/expand the visibility of the slides in that section.

Creating a section

2.3.2 Modify slide order

As presentations are being developed, or as they are updated over time, they often need to be reorganized.

Modify slide order:

1.   On the View tab, select Slide Sorter to change the view mode
2.   Select one or more slides
3.   Click and drag the left mouse button to a new location

Slides can also be repositioned in the left slide thumbnail area while in Normal view mode.

Adjusting slide order

2.3.3 Rename sections

Sections may be renamed at any time, not just when they are first created.

Rename sections:

1. Right-click on a section name and select **Rename Section**
2. Enter a new name and click the Rename button

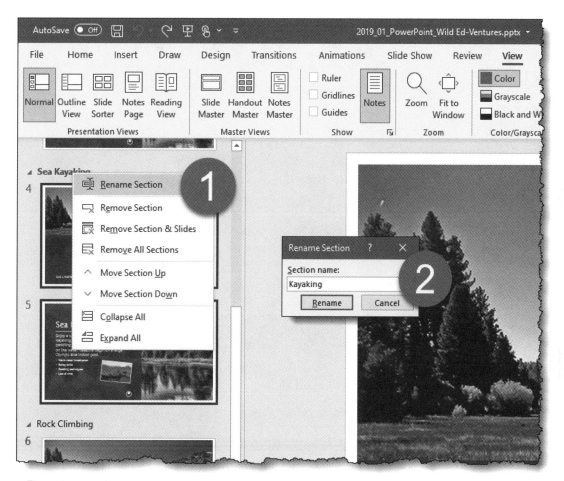

Renaming a section

2.4 Practice tasks

Try the topics covered in this chapter to make sure you understand the concepts. These tasks are sequential and should be completed in the same Word document unless noted otherwise. Saving the results is optional, unless assigned by an instructor.

First Step:

✓ Open provided document **Wild Ed-Ventures.pptx**

Task 1.1:

✓ Select slide #2 and add a section named **Day Camp & Parties**.

Task 1.2

✓ Insert a **Summary Zoom** Slide using the default selected sections.

Task 1.3

✓ Duplicate slide # 8, the Rock Climbing slide with picture of rock climber.

Task 1.4:

✓ Hide slide # 8, the Rock Climbing slide with picture of rock climber.

Task 1.5:

✓ Add custom footer text "Draft" to all slides.

2.5 Self-exam & review questions

Self-Exam:

The following questions can be used to check your knowledge of this chapter. The answers can be found at the bottom of the next page.

1. Slides can be created by importing a Word document. (T/F)
2. A slide layout can only be selected after creating a new slide. (T/F)
3. The summary zoom slide is placed right after the title slide. (T/F)
4. In addition to Date & Time and custom text, what else can be shown in the foot? _____.
5. Sections can be collapsed to hide thumbnail views. (T/F)

Review Questions:

The following questions may be assigned by your instructor to assess your knowledge of this chapter. Your instructor has the answers to the review questions.

1. When importing Word outlines, Title and Heading 1 styles are separate slides. (T/F)
2. To import slides from another presentation, both presentations must be open. (T/F)
3. The slide layout can be changed by right-clicking on a slide thumbnail view. (T/F)
4. A summary Zoom slide provides an interactive way to navigate a presentation. (T/F)
5. Slides with content may not be duplicated. (T/F)
6. Presentations with a large file size should not be emailed. (T/F)
7. Which tab is Format Background found on? _____ .
8. Sections cannot be renamed once they have been created. (T/F)
9. There is more than one way to reorder slides. (T/F)
10. Hidden slides are still visible in the thumbnail view, but not during a presentation. (T/F)

Notes:

3 Insert and Format Text, Shapes, and Images

Introduction

This chapter covers the essential tasks related to adding, and working with, content in your presentation. Text, shapes, and images are often the primary ingredient within a presentation. Learn how to add and manage this content for a successful presentation.

3.0 Manage text

It is important to understand how to manage text within a presentation. This section covers the required steps to select, move, copy, and delete text.

3.0.0 Select text

At times, text in PowerPoint can be difficult to select when layered with (above/below) other elements like pictures, shapes, and other text. Moving other elements out of the way is not required when one knows how to quickly select using the Tab key.

Selecting text using the Tab key:

1. Press the Esc key twice to unselect anything that may be selected
2. Place the cursor over the element to be selected
3. Tap the Tab key until the desired element highlights
   a. In this example, the image and another text element highlight first
4. Move the cursor over an edge of the highlighted textbox and click

The text is now selected and may be moved, copied, or deleted per this section.

Selecting overlapping text

3.0.1 Move text

Text can be moved by dragging with the mouse or using the arrow keys on the keyboard. While dragging, PowerPoint offers various alignment references to adjacent elements. Using the arrows supports a finer level of adjustment based on visual preference.

Move text using arrow keys:

1. Select the desired text
2. Use any of the arrow keys to nudge the text in one of four directions
   a. Press and hold to move continuously
   b. Tap the arrow key to move in small increments

Move text by dragging with mouse:

1. Select the desired text
2. Click and drag on one of the edges of the textbox (using left mouse button)
3. Optional: While dragging text, watch for alignments with adjacent elements
   a. The image below shows a vertical dashed line, indicating a horizontal alignment with the text above
4. Release mouse button to position text

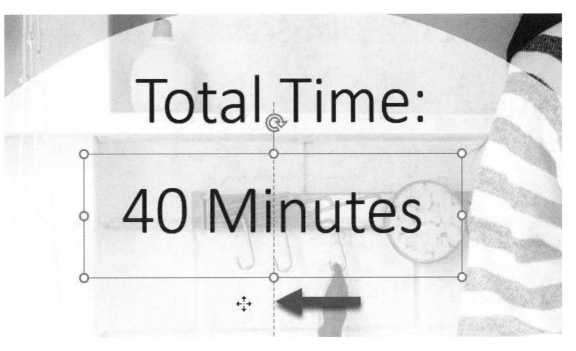

Text alignment reference with adjacent text

3.0.2 Copy text

Text can be copied using the standard Windows Copy and Paste workflow. It is also possible to copy text by dragging it, while also holding down the Ctrl key. Finally, a third option exists, called Duplicate, which results in a copy of the selected element being positioned right next to the original element.

Copy text using Copy/Paste:

Use this option when needing to copy content to another slide within a presentation.

1. Select the desired text
2. Select **Home → Copy** (drop-down) **→ Copy** (or **Ctrl + C**)
3. Near the desired location, select **Home → Paste** (drop-down) **:**
    a. **Use Destination Theme**
       Pasted text will match format of adjacent text
    b. **Picture**
       Pasted text becomes an image where text cannot be edited
    c. **Ctrl+V**
       Paste text at current cursor location
4. Move copied text as needed

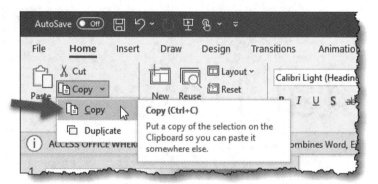

Copy selected text to clipboard

Copy text using Ctrl + drag:

1. Select the desired text
2. While holding the Ctrl yet, click and drag text to copy

Copy text using Duplicate:

1. Select the desired text
2. Click **Home → Copy** (drop-down) **→ Duplicate** (see image above)
3. Move duplicated text as needed

3.0.3 Delete text

When text is no longer needed on a slide, there are two ways to delete it. Both are eventually permanent, and the text cannot be retrieved.

Delete text using Del key:

1. Select the desired text
2. Press the **Del** key on the keyboard

Delete text using Cut to Clipboard:

When text is cut to the clipboard, it is deleted and saved in the Window clipboard until pasted, or until something else is copied/cut to the clipboard.

1. Select the desired text
2. Select **Home → Cut** (or Ctrl + X)

The previous steps cover deleting the entire text object. To delete portions of text within the textbox or shape, see the next topic on entering text.

3.1 Format text

Formatting text is important to make your message clear to the audience. This section will look at how to change the look (styles), organize into columns, as well as lists.

3.1.0 Enter text

Text may be entered into previously created shapes and textboxes. It is important to know how to select these elements, which is the same for selecting text, covered previously in this chapter. Later in this chapter, the process of creating shapes and text boxes is covered.

Enter, or edit, text in a textbox:

1. Click within textbox and enter/edit text
2. Optional: If elements are layers, use the **Tab** select method (previously covered for selecting text) and then right-click on select **Edit Text**

Enter, or edit, text in a shape:

1. Right-click on shape
2. Select **Edit Text**
3. Enter/edit text as desired

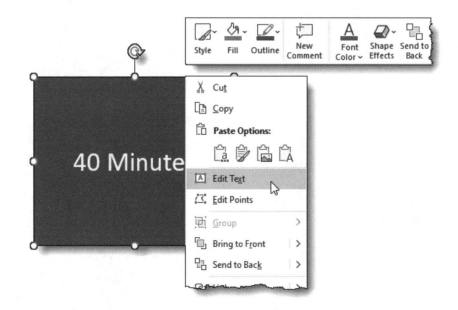

Enter/edit text in presentation

3.1.1 Apply formatting and styles to text

Given the way PowerPoint Themes control much of the formatting in a presentation, there are no text styles like Microsoft Word. However, there are still many ways in which text may be modified for specific requirements.

Here are the ways text may be modified:

- **Font**
  - Font style; Regular, Italic, Bold, Bold Italic
  - Size
  - Color
  - Underline style
  - Effects; Strikethrough, Small caps, etc.
- **Paragraph**
  - Alignment: Left, Center, Right, Justified, Distributed
  - Indentation
  - Spacing
- Rotation
- WordArt styles

Many of these setting can be accessed by right-clicking on selected text and picking Font or Paragraph to access the dialogs shown below.

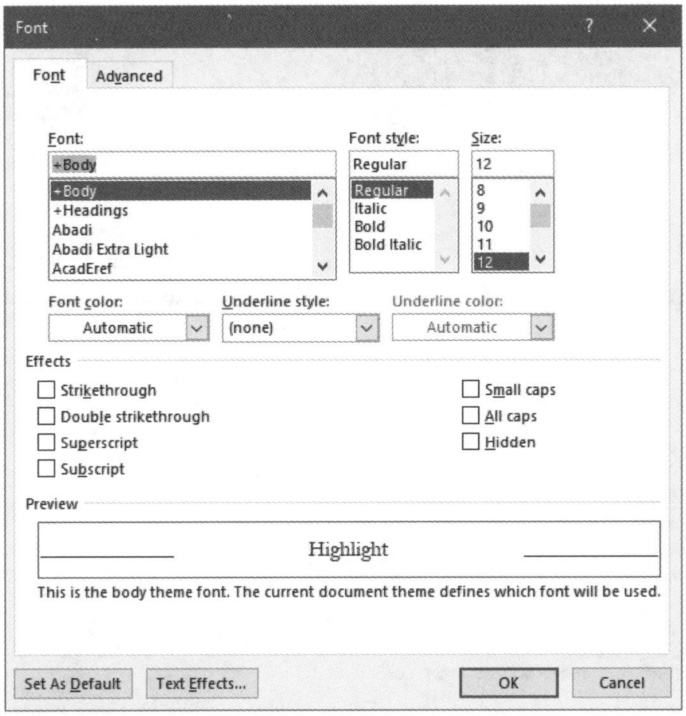

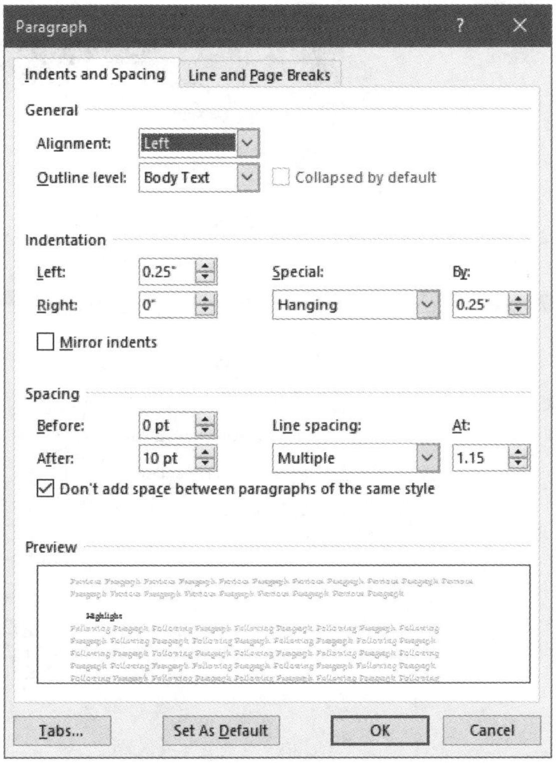

Font and paragraph properties for selected text

There are too many ways to modify text to show here. However, they all involve selecting the text and trying various options until a desired outcome is achieved. If a change is not what was hoped for, simply click Undo and try something else.

Apply formatting and styles to text:

1. Select text
2. Apply styles:
    a. **Home** tab
        - Edit Font style, size, color, etc.
    b. **Shape Format** tab
        - Rotation, WordArt styles, etc.
    c. Right-click → **Format shape** (opens side pane, see image to right)
        - Fill and Line tab
        - Effects
        - Size & Properties

The image below shows the Advanced tab, found in the Fonts dialog shown on the previous page.

Format shape pane

Advanced tab in the Fonts dialog

3.1.2 Format text in multiple columns

If needed, text can be formatted into columns to better organize the content.

Format text into multiple columns:

1. Select text, shape, or textbox
2. Pick **Home → Add or Remove Columns** (drop-down) → **Two Columns**
   a. Optional: **Select More Columns**, enter a number, and click **Ok**
3. Review results

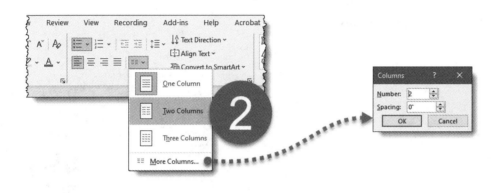

Formatting text into multiple columns

3.1.3 Create bulleted and numbered lists

Formatting text into a list can help the individual points be easier to read and understand.

Create bulleted and numbered lists:

1. Select text, shape, or textbox
2. Pick **Home → Bullets**
    a. Optional: click Bullets drop-down for more options
3. Review results

The steps are the same for a numbered list. In the Bullets/Number drop-down lists, pick the **Bullets and Numbering…** command for more options.

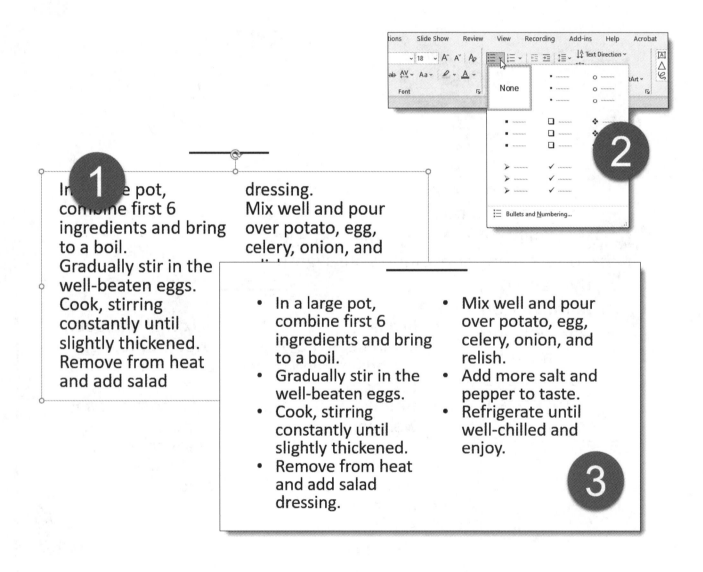

3.2 Insert links

Presentations can have links to other locations with a document, as well as to external web pages on the internet.

3.2.0 Introduction

PowerPoint allows text and images to host links to other slides within the document. This can be helpful if your audience asks specific questions and requires the conversation to go in a different direction. Rather than quickly jumping through a bunch of slides, you can click a link and jump past to another slide.

Another option is to insert a hyperlink to an external website. Clicking one of these links opens a browser and shows the web page. The challenges to keep in mind are that that you must have access to the internet during the presentation. Also, keep in mind that web sites are changing all the time. Be sure to review web pages just prior to a presentation to validate the content.

3.2.1 Insert hyperlinks

Hyperlinks are convenient links to other slides and external content, such as websites.

Insert hyperlink – Web Page:

1. Select text within shape or textbox, **Right-click → Link**
2. Select **Web Page** on left
3. Enter **address** (url) and click **OK**

Creating hyperlink to web page

Another option is to link to another slide within the presentation. Rather than picking Web Page in the previous steps, select **Place in This Document**. Now, pick from the slides listed within the list on the right.

Creating hyperlink to another location within presentation

3.2.2 Insert Section Zoom links and Slide Zoom links

To make a presentation more interactive, Zoom links can be added that provide a quick way to jump to a section or a slide.

Insert Section Zoom links:

1. Select a slide to insert Section Zoom links on
2. Click **Insert → Zoom → Section Zoom**
3. Select Sections to insert
4. Move/position link images on slide

The same steps can be followed, selecting Slide Zoom (rather than Section Zoom) to insert links to slides rather than sections.

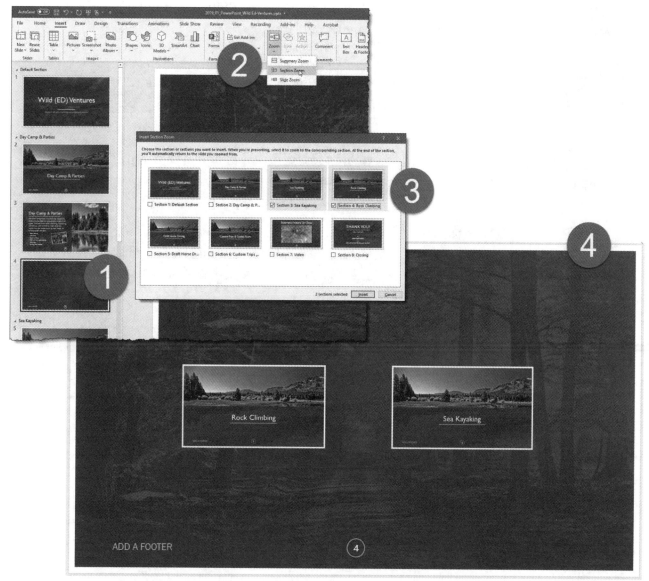

Inserting Slide or Section Zoom links onto current slide

3.3 Insert and format images

This section starts with a high-level introduction to the features covered in this chapter.

3.3.0 Introduction

PowerPoint offers many graphical elements on the Insert tab. The following list is a brief introduction of what they are and when to use them.

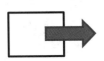

Picture   *used to include a photograph*

Inserts raster image (e.g. a **jpg** or **png** file) which could be computer generated or a photograph. PowerPoint also provides access to an online library of stock images. When selected, use the **Picture Format** tab to edit size, artistic effects, transparency, and more.

Shapes   *used to stylize the presentation or graphically define a sidebar*

Create ready-made shapes such as circles, squares, lines and more. When selected, use the **Shape Format** tab to modify size, color and more.

Icons   *used to visually group ideas or sections of information*

Places a highly stylized graphic used to visually communicate using symbols. When selected, use the **Graphics Format** tab to modify size, color, and more.

3D Models   *used to create interactive presentation and reduce number of static pictures*

Inserts a 3D model which can be viewed from any angle by clicking and dragging the cursor over the object. When selected, use the **3D Model** tab to modify size, view, and more.

SmartArt   *manage complex graphics consisting of multiple interconnected shapes*

SmartArt are intelligent interconnected graphics used to describe workflows, processes, and more. When selected, use the **SmartArt Design** and **Format** tabs to modify styles, layouts, graphics, and more.

Chart   *used to convey data graphically*

Inserts a bar, area, or line chart to graphically display data. When selected, use the **Chart Styles** and **Format** tabs to modify styles, data, and more.

Screenshot   *used to capture information on the computer screen*

This tool is used to capture graphics currently displayed on the screen, in any application. The result is a picture element.

3.3.1 Resize and crop images

Images can often say a lot more than words, making them key to a good presentation. Thus, it is important to know the steps required to resize and crop them.

Resize image:

An image often comes in too large and needs to be resized on the slide.

1. Select an image on the current slide
2. Adjust image size in one of two ways:
   a. Click and drag on corner/edge grips to dynamically change size
   b. Click **Picture Format** tab and edit Height/Width parameters

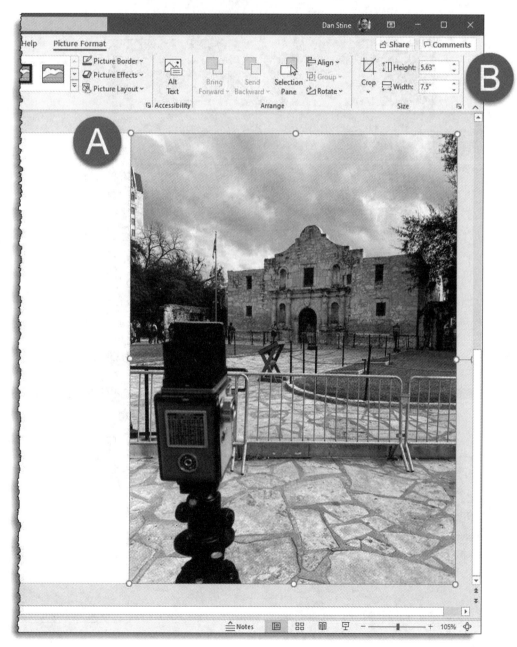

Resizing an image

Crop image:

Crop hide a portion of the selected image. This is a non-destructive process, meaning the hidden portion is not deleted, and can be exposed at any point in the future.

1. With image selected, click **Picture Format → Crop**
2. Drag on corner/edge grips to dynamically crop image

Cropping an image

3.3.2 Apply built-in styles and effects to images

PowerPoint offers several tools to manipulate images to make them stand out or improve the aesthetic quality of the overall slide. Styles and effects are non-destructive, to the original image, and may be removed at any time.

Apply Picture Styles:

A picture style applies multiple picture effects at once.

1. Select an image on the current slide
2. Click **Picture Format → Picture Styles → Select an option**, e.g. Bevel Perspective

Applying a picture style to an image

Apply Picture Effects:

Enhance an image with an effect, such as shadows, reflections, glow, soft edges, and more.

1. Select the image you wish to enhance with a picture effect
2. Click **Picture Format → Picture Effects → Select an option**, e.g. Soft Edge, 25 Point

▌ Each effect has a name, which appears in a tooltip as shown in the image below

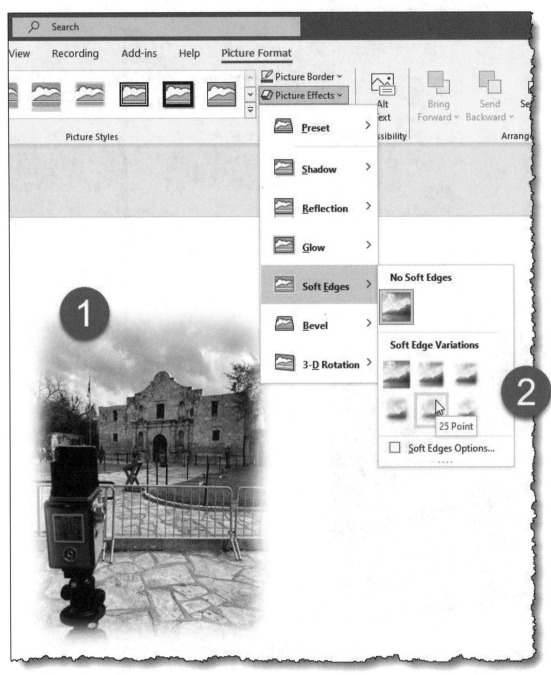

Applying a picture effect to an image

Apply artistic effect:

1. Select the image you wish to enhance with an artistic effect
2. Click **Picture Format → Artistic Effects → Select an option**, e.g. Pencil Sketch

> Each effect has a name, which appears in a tooltip as shown in the image below.

Applying an artistic effect to an image

The Picture Format tab has additional options to adjust an image. Most work in a similar way to what was covered above. Try inserting an image into PowerPoint and apply various styles and effects to explore the options.

3.3.3 Insert screenshots and screen clippings

The steps to insert a representation of current content on your screen is covered here.

Insert Screenshot:

Insert the full view of another application, currently open, on the current slide.

1. Select slide to place screenshot on, i.e. make it current
2. **Insert → Screenshot**; select from available window previews
   a. Available Windows are based on all open applications on-screen currently

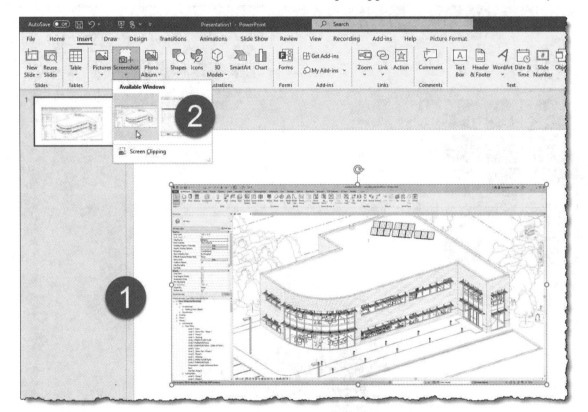

Insert screenshot

Insert Screen Clipping: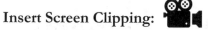

Insert a selected area of the current screen graphics on the current slide.

1. Select slide to place screenshot on, i.e. make it current
2. **Insert → Screenshot → Screen Clipping**
3. On your computer screen(s), click and drag to select an area to capture

The area highlighted is now placed in the document as a static image. Use PowerPoint's image crop tool to further refine the clipped area (which results in a smaller image).

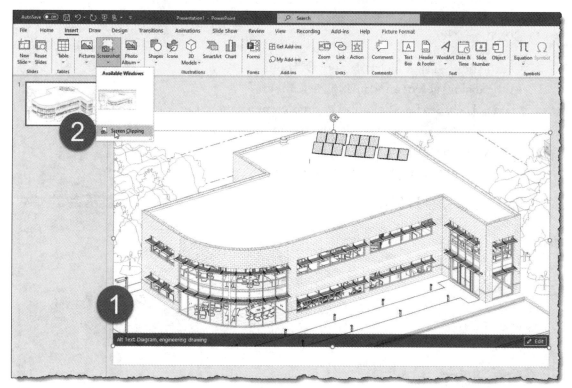

Insert screen clipping

3.4 Insert & format graphic elements

Graphic elements, such as shapes and text boxes, can be positioned in several ways within a document. Many of these options will be covered in this section.

3.4.0 Introduction

PowerPoint offers highly stylized icons which can be used to represent ideas graphically.

Insert Icons:

1. On the desired slide, select **Insert → Icons**
2. In the dialog, **select** an icon and click **Insert**
    a. Use search to help find desired graphics more quickly
    b. Notice the other tabs at the top of the dialog: e.g. Cutout People, etc.
3. Review results
    a. In this example, the icons were resized and positioned side-by-side.

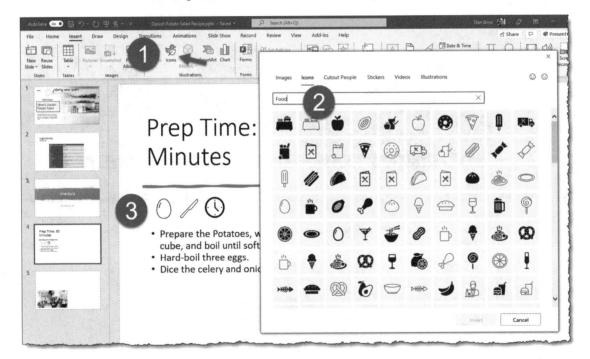

Inserting an icon

3.4.1 Insert and change shapes

PowerPoint offers many shapes to enhance graphical communication with your audience.

Insert shapes:

1. **Insert → Shapes → Select a shape**, e.g. Star: 5 Points
2. In desired location, click and drag diagonally to define shape size
   a. Hold down the Shift key to lock proportions while dragging

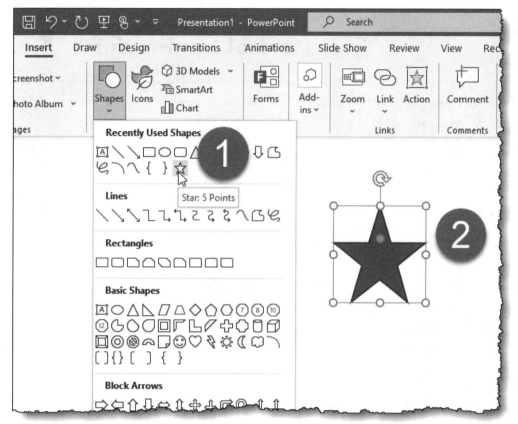

Inserting a shape

Whenever the shape is selected control grips appear which facilitate the following changes:

Rotation: Click and drag the rotation-icon to adjust the shape angle

Stretch: click and drag one of the edge-grips to distort the shape

Manipulate: Click and drag the gold-grip to resize the shape internally

Layout Options: Click the layout options icon to open the menu, then select an option

> **Tip:** Holding the Shift key does the following: snaps to rotation increments *and* locks the proportions when dragging a corner grip.

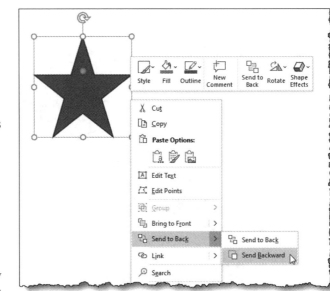

Change a shape: Select a shape and click **Shape Format** (tab) → **Edit Shape** → **Change Shape**. Select a new option from the list.

Finally, the **Shape Format** tab has many additional options to modify the selected shape. Knowing how to modify a shape can save time during the certification exam, compared to deleting an element and starting over.

3.4.2 Draw by using digital ink

Drawing on a slide facilitates presentation design comments and capturing audience feedback. Although digital ink can be accomplished with a mouse, a stylus-enabled touchscreen or tablet is the ideal use case.

Adding digital ink:

1. Select **Draw → Drawing Tools → Select a tool**, e.g. Red pen
2. Using a stylus, or mouse, draw in the current slide

Draw on-screen using digital ink tools

Clicking the down-arrow, associated with each draw tool, opens a selection of line thickness and color options as shown to the right.

Clicking the cursor icon, at the far left of the Draw tab, switches from the selected pen back to select mode. This allows drawn elements to be selected. When a digital ink element is select, the convert options on the Ribbon can be used to turn the drawing into shapes and/or text.

3.4.3 Add text to shapes and text boxes

Know how to add and modify text within a shape or textbox.

Add and modify text in shapes:

1. Select a shape element
2. Right-click and select **Edit Text**
3. Enter text and review results

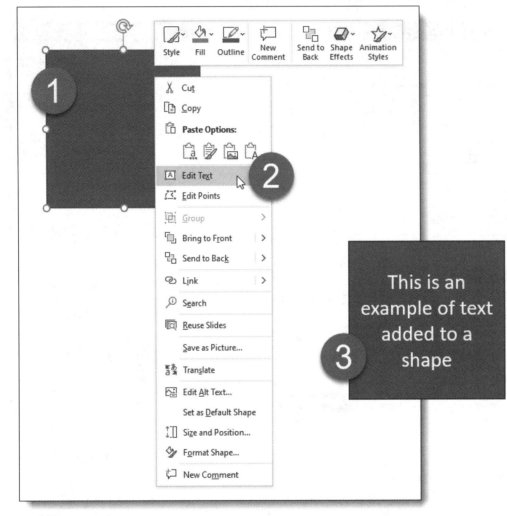

Add text to a shape

Similar to editing a text box, text within a shape can be edited just like all other text in PowerPoint.

3.4.4 Resize shapes and text boxes

Most graphic elements may be selected and resized by dragging the corner or edge grips on-screen. If more accuracy is required, typing in a specific height and/or width is also possible.

Resize a shape (or text box):

- A. With the graphic selected, edit the width or height on the element's 'format' tab, Shape Format example shown below.
- B. For even more control, click the dialog icon (lower right corner) of the size panel. Here, a percentage may be used to resize the image. The aspect ratio can also be unlocked, to allow the image to be distorted.

Resizing a shape element

3.4.5 Format shapes and text boxes

Shapes and text boxes may be selected and formatted in various ways, from size, shape, and fill properties to text content and rotation. Add text is covered on the previous page.

Format a shape (or text box):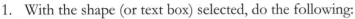

1. With the shape (or text box) selected, do the following:
   A. Use the various options on the element's 'format' tab, Shape Format example shown below.
   B. Alternatively, right-click the shape (or text box) and select Format Shape.

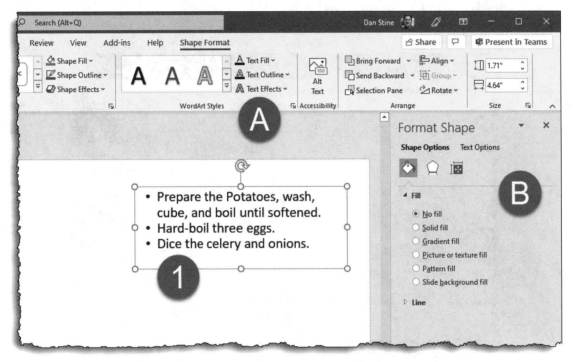

Formatting shape element

Formatting options include:

- **Shape Fill**   Fill extents of shape with color, picture, gradient, texture
- **Shape Outline**   Define the color, width, and line style for the shape edge
- **Shape Effects**   Apply a shadow, glow, reflection, 3D rotation to shape
- **Shape Styles**   *Apply a collection of settings listed above (see next page)*
- **Text Fill**   Fill font with color, picture, gradient, texture
- **Text Outline**   Define the color, width, and line style for the font edge
- **Text Effects**   Apply a shadow, glow, reflection, 3D rotation to text
- **Arrange**   Move selected elements into alignment with each other
- **Size**   Adjust dimensions of shape. See previous page
- **Text Styles**   *Apply a collection of settings listed above (see next page)*

3.4.6 Apply built-in styles to shapes and text boxes

Shape and text styles may be used to quickly apply a collection of formatting options.

Apply built-in styles to a shape:

1. Select the desired shape to modify
2. On the Shape Format tab, select a Shape Style from the list

Notice, when hovering over a style a style name appears. This is important to know, as the certification exam may specify a specific named style to apply.

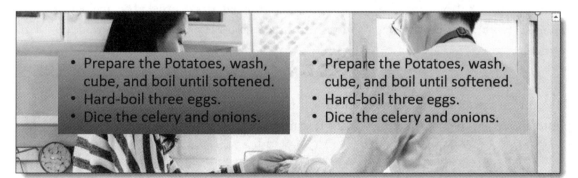

Applying built-in shape styles

The styles with a checkerboard background have a transparent background, allowing graphics and images behind to remain partially visible. Similarly, a color fill preview with a checkboard pattern will result in a semi-transparent color being used to fill the shape.

Style examples: solid gradient fill and semi-transparent color filles

3.4.7 Add alt text to graphic elements for accessibility

It is important to add Alt Text to graphic elements, images and shapes, to help people who are blind or have low vision experience the presentation. When someone uses a screen reader, they will read the alt text, in addition to the main text on the slide, to help visualize the full context of the material. The Alt Text is not visible.

Add Alt Text to an image (or graphic element):

1. Select the desired image or graphic element
    a. Right-click and select Edit Alt Text…
2. In the Alt Text pane, type 1-2 sentences that describe the element

Adding alt text to an element

Notice, in the Alt Text pane, there is an option to **Mark as decorative**. This will let the reader know they are not missing anything important, and the element is simply added for an aesthetic effect.

Another option is to select **Generate a description automatically**. The results for the photo above are shown to the right. This text may be modified or expounded upon.

A person holding a person's hand in a kitchen

Description automatically generated with low confidence

3.5 Order and group objects on slides

Once content is curated and placed on a slide, PowerPoint offers several tools to graphically enhance the position of elements that are next to each other or even overlapping. This includes aligning edges and controlling front to back positioning.

3.5.0 Introduction

Understanding how to select objects can make editing content a lot easier, especially when they overlap. The first thing to know is you can tap (not hold down) the Tab key to temporarily highlight elements beneath your cursor. When the element you wish to select is highlight, click to select it.

Note these selection options, as shown in the image below:

A. From the Home tab, on the Ribbon, it is also possible to select all elements on the current slide.

B. Using the Selection Pane, we can see which elements are selected, or select items in the pane to also select them on the slide.

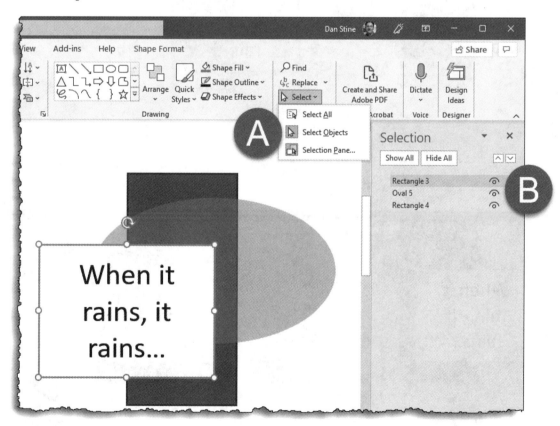

Selection options

3.5.1 Order shapes, images, and text boxes

Graphic elements are stacked on top of each other in the order they were added to the presentation. Occasionally this order needs to be adjusted, especially for text, e.g. moving it to the top so it can be seen/read by the audience.

Order shapes and a text box: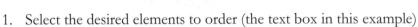

1. Select the desired elements to order (the text box in this example)
2. Right-click and select **Bring to Front** (not the arrow)
3. Select a shape to order (the transparent oval in this example)
    a. Right-click and select **Bring to Front** → **Bring Forward**
    b. FYI: selecting *Bring to Front* here would have covered the text
4. Review the results

The **Send to Back** and **Send Backward** each work in a similar way.

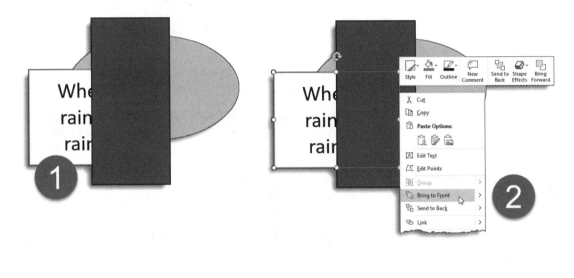

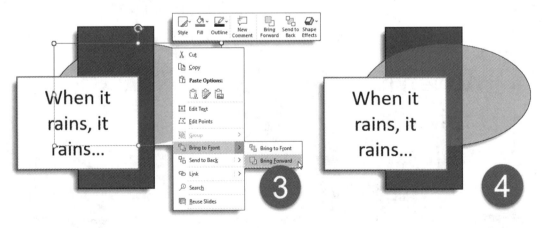

Using Bring to Front and Bring Forward

3.5.2 Align shapes, images, and text boxes

The graphic layout of a slide often looks better when elements are aligned. When they are off, especially just a small amount, it can be distracting to the audience. Note that the alignment is not maintained, it is a one-time adjustment to the selected elements.

Align graphic elements:

5. Select the desired elements to align (images and text box in this example)
6. On Select Picture Format → Align Top
7. Review results

Experiment with the other options to better understand how they work.

Using the align tool

Align tool results

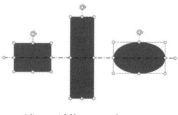

Align middle example

3.5.3 Group shapes and images

Multiple graphic elements can be grouped together, which maintains their composition and makes it easier to move, as they now act like a single element.

Grouping graphic elements: 🎥

1. Select the desired elements to group (two shapes and a text box in this example)
2. Right-click and select **Group → Group**

The elements now act like a single element when selected. Once elements are grouped, they may be ungrouped following the same steps and selecting Ungroup as seen in the image below.

Grouping graphic elements

3.5.4 Display alignment tools

When dragging elements on-screen using the mouse, various alignment references present themselves. These may be used to manually align graphical elements.

In the example shown below, the oval is being dragged upward and an alignment reference is showing where the top of the oval will align with the adjacent rectangle. Releasing the mouse at this point will result in the two elements being perfectly aligned.

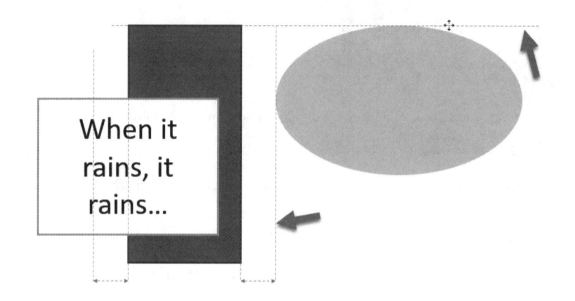

Using on-screen alignment references

3.6 Practice tasks

Try the topics covered in this chapter to make sure you understand the concepts. These tasks are sequential and should be completed in the same Word document unless noted otherwise. Saving the results is optional, unless assigned by an instructor.

First Step:

- ✓ Open provided document **Course Flyer.pptx**

Task 1.1:

- ✓ On the second slide, select the text hidden in the image and move it on top.

Task 1.2

- ✓ On the third slide, edit the two sets of elements on the left to match the required results shown on the right.

Task 1.3

- ✓ On the second slide, adjust the text (beneath the title 'Topics Covered') to be a bulleted list.

Task 1.4:

- ✓ On the second slide, add the following Picture Effect: Soft Edge – 10 Point.

Task 1.5:

- ✓ On the fourth slide, add a screen clipping of a portion of your computer's desktop.

3.7 Self-exam & review questions

Self-Exam:

The following questions can be used to check your knowledge of this chapter. The answers can be found at the bottom of the next page.

1. Selected text can be moved using the arrow keys. (T/F)
2. Only a text box can contain text. (T/F)
3. The Add Columns tools is found on the Home tab. (T/F)
4. Command used to hide a portion of an image? _____.
5. Zoom links create an interactive presentation. (T/F)

Review Questions:

The following questions may be assigned by your instructor to assess your knowledge of this chapter. Your instructor has the answers to the review questions.

1. Text can only be copied using the clipboard. (T/F)
2. Add text to a shape by right-click → edit text. (T/F)
3. Zoom links are created from the Insert tab on the Ribbon. (T/F)
4. The crop tool permanently deletes a portion of the image. (T/F)
5. Picture effects can be undone (removed) at any time. (T/F)
6. A text box can be resized from the format tab or by dragging its edge. (T/F)
7. Which command helps those who are blind or have low vision better understand images within a presentation? _____ _____ .
8. Elements overlap other elements based on the order added to presentation. (T/F)
9. The alignment tools will continuously keep elements aligned. (T/F)
10. Grouped elements act and move like a single element. (T/F)

Notes:

4 Insert Tables, Charts, SmartArt, 3D Models, and Media

4.0 Introduction to tables and lists

Before learning how to create and manage tables and lists it is helpful to understand what they are, in the context of PowerPoint, and why they are needed.

4.0.0 Tables defined

Tables are mainly used to organize information, like how Microsoft Excel is used, but within a presentation that is primarily sentences. Notice the two examples below, where the text on the left is not aligned when using the same number of tabs on each line. It is possible to get the information to align but takes an ongoing effort. For example, everything could align until the last line, which requires going back and adjusting all previous lines by adding another tab.

Conversely, the table in the example on the right will always align and can easily by adjusted by dragging the column spacing. Additionally, tables have formatting options to right align a column to, for example, align the decimal place in currency.

Monday　　→　　3:00·pm¶

Tuesday　　→　　9:00·am¶

Wednesday →　10:00·am¶

Thursday　→　　1:30·pm¶

Friday→12:00·pm¶

Saturday/Sunday　→　Closed¶

Monday	3:00 pm
Tuesday	9:00 am
Wednesday	10:00 am
Thursday	1:30 pm
Friday	12:00 pm
Saturday/Sunday	Closed

Data organized with tabs　　　　　　*Data organized within a table*

4.0.1 Lists defined

Lists are used to organize a single column of information, such as steps, table of contents, ingredients, etc. The main options are Numbered or Bulleted. Numbered can be numbers, letters or a combination as shown in the two examples on the left, below. Bulleted lists use graphics, like the dot/circles shown below. A numbered list is preferred if the list represents a specific order. The **Decrease/Increase Indent** buttons are used to control list hierarchy.

A. Days of Operation
   a. Monday
   b. Wednesday
   c. Thursday
   d. Friday
   e. Saturday/Sunday

1. Days of Operation
   a. Monday
   b. Wednesday
   c. Thursday
   d. Friday
   e. Saturday/Sunday

• Days of Operation
   o Monday
   o Wednesday
   o Thursday
   o Friday
   o Saturday/Sunday

List examples

4.1 Insert and format tables

Review the steps required to create tables in the current presentation.

4.1.0 Introduction

Once a table has been created, or selected, there are many tools available to edit them. Before some of these workflows are covered in this section, it is helpful to know how these tools are accessed.

Clicking within, or selecting, a table reveals two tabs on the Ribbon; they are:

- Table Design
- Layout

These tabs, and a portion of their contents, are shown below.

Table Design and Layout tabs – shown when a table is selected

Some tools are applied to the entire table, like the table styles options. Others are applied to the selected portion of the table, such as a cell, row, or column.

Here is a little more detail about each tab:

Table Design
The tools on the Table Design tab are used to select a table style, table style options, and control how the lines making up the table appear (i.e. borders).

Layout
The tools on the Layout tab facilitate inserting, splitting, and even deleting table cells, rows, and/or columns. Here, it is also possible to control the size of a cell, row, and/or column as well as the text justification. Unlike Word and Excel, PowerPoint does not facilitate sorting that data or using formulas.

4.1.1 Create and insert tables

Review the steps required to create a new table with a specific number of rows and columns.

Create a new table:

1. Select the slide the table will be placed on
2. Click **Insert** → **Table** drop-down list
3. Do one of the following:
   a. Move the cursor across the cells to define the desired table size, *or*
   b. Click Insert Table… and manually enter number of rows/columns

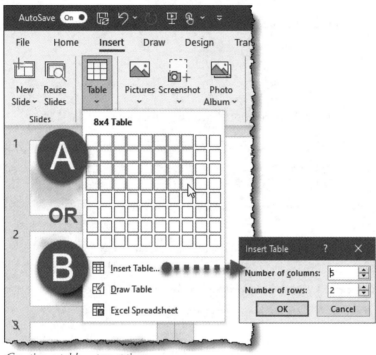

Creating a table – two options

The result is a blank table with the specified number of rows and columns, as shown below. The table can then be moved around on the current slide.

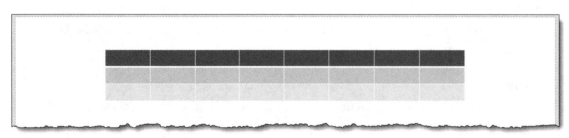

Empty new table created

Another way to create a table is by copying an existing table from the current document or another open PowerPoint document. This might be done if using the same information in multiple presentations, or if the formatting is the same. In the latter example, the text is modified, and the formatting is kept intact, which might save time for a heavily formatted table. Formatting might include shaded columns/rows, font variations, hidden/dashed lines, etc.

Copy a table:

1. Hover over a table
2. Select the table's edge; grips will appear as shown below (no table cells are selected)
3. Copy to clipboard using **Ctrl + C**
4. Switch to another slide or presentation
5. Paste from clipboard using **Ctrl + V**

Name	Role	Salary	Years of Experience
Rachel Johnson	Architect	$85k	8
Joe Billman	Structural Engineer	$80k	6
Martin Hepler	Civil Engineer	$110K	26
Sarah Burden	Mechanical Engineer	$94k	14
Ben Smith	Electrical Engineer	$90k	8

Copied table

The copied table has no connection to the original table. Thus, changes to the new table will not affect the original table, and vice versa.

4.1.2 Insert and delete table rows and columns

Once a table is created, rows and/or columns often need to be added or removed.

Insert a Row Below:

1. Click within a row
2. Click **Layout → Insert Below**
3. Review the results; a new row is created below the selected cell

New row added below selected row/cell

Delete a Column:

1. Click within a column
2. Click **Layout → Delete → Delete Column**
3. Review the results; the selected column is deleted

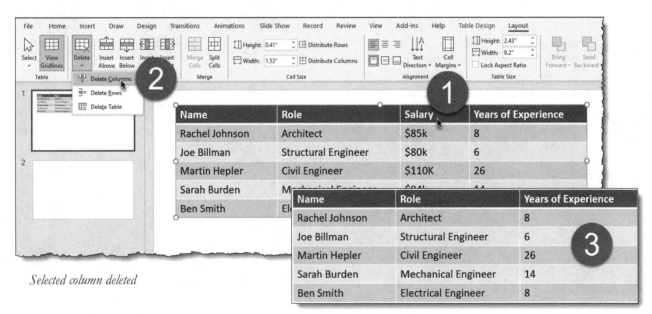

Selected column deleted

4.1.3 Apply built-in table styles

PowerPoint provides several built-in styles to quickly format a selected table.

Apply built-in table style:

1. Select a table
2. Click **Table Design → Table Styles** and select an option
   Tip: notice a style name appears when hovering the cursor above
3. Review the results

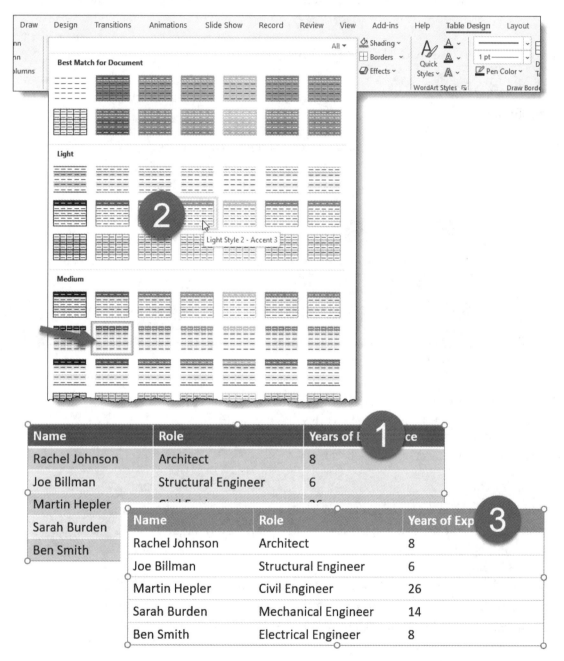

Applying a built-in table style

4.2 Insert and modify charts

Review the steps required to create charts in the current presentation.

4.2.0 Introduction

Once a chart has been created, or selected, there are many tools available to edit them. Before some of these workflows are covered in this section, it is helpful to know how these tools are accessed.

Selecting a chart reveals two tabs on the Ribbon; they are:

- Chart Design
- Format

These tabs, and a portion of their contents, are shown below.

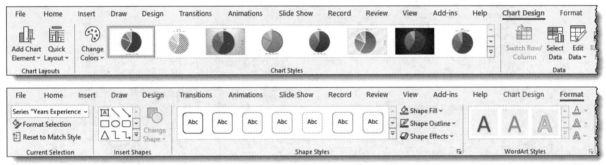

Chart Design and Format tabs – shown when a chart is selected

Some tools are applied to the entire chart, like the chart styles options. Others are applied to the selected portion of the chart, such as the title text font.

Here is a little more detail about each tab:

<u>Chart Design</u>
The tools on the Chart Design tab are used to select a chart style, chart layout options, and edit the data (via spreadsheet pop-up view) that defines the chart.

<u>Format</u>
The tools on the Format tab facilitate inserting shapes associated with the chart. A selected shape within the chart can also have a unique Shape Style applied to make it stand out. Selected text can also have WordArt Styles applied.

4.2.1 Create and insert charts

Charts are a great way to convey information quickly and PowerPoint offers several styles.

Create a pie chart:

1. On the desired slide, select **Insert → Chart**
2. In the Insert Chart dialog, select the chart style/options and click **OK**
3. In the pop-up spreadsheet, edit columns A and B
   Tip: drag the selection window down to include more rows
4. Review the result and reposition the chart

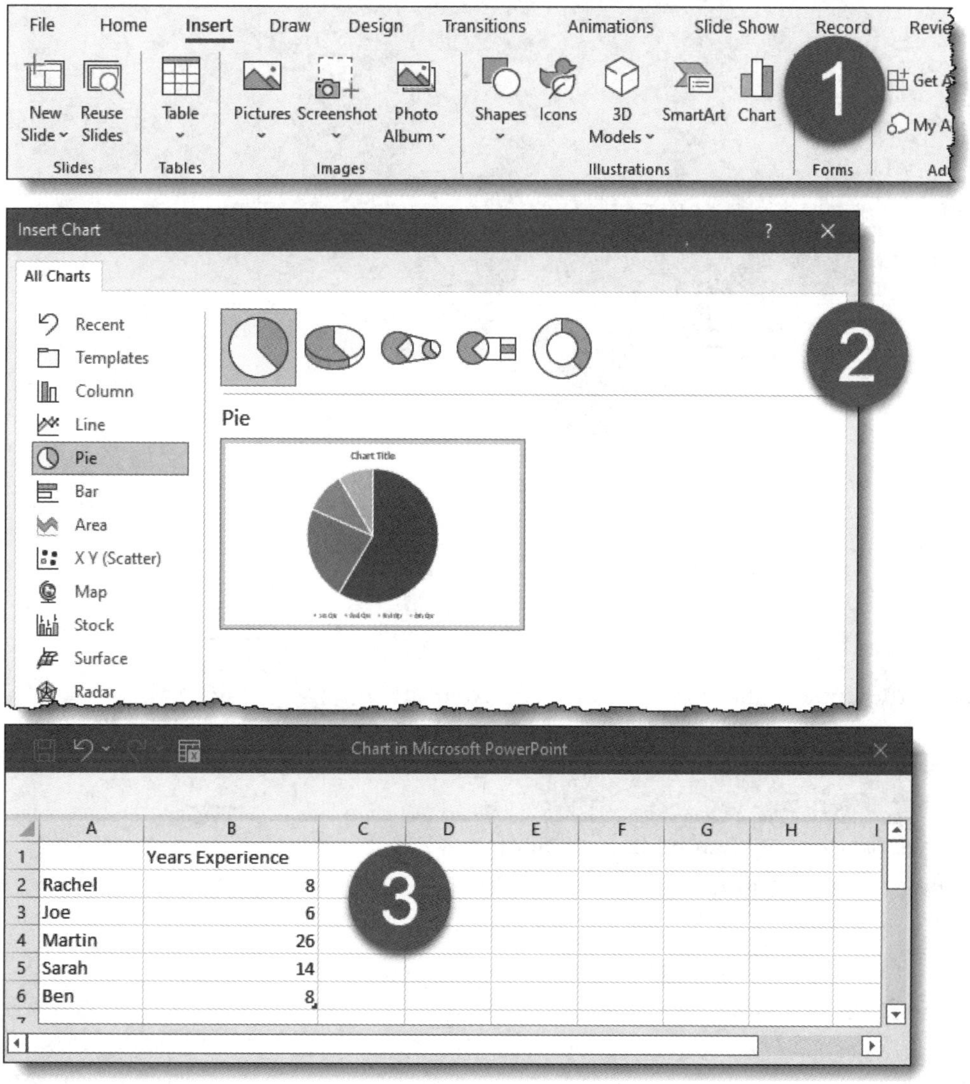

Inserting a pie chart

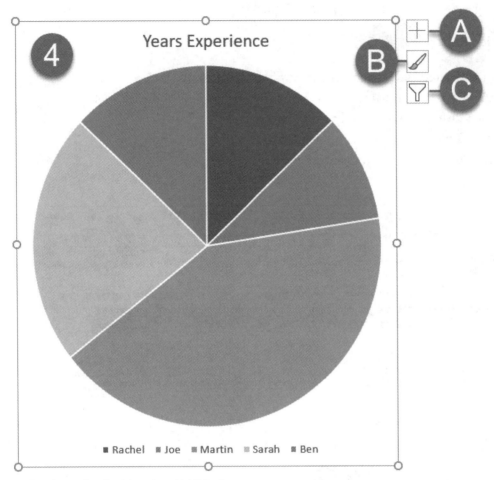

Pie chart selected, with options highlighted

When a chart is selected, there are three icons/tools available in the upper right corner, as highlighted in the image above. Here is what each does:

A. **Chart Elements**
   Add, remove, or change chart elements such as the title, legend, gridlines, and data labels.
B. **Chart Styles**
   Set a style and color scheme for the selected chart.
C. **Chart Filters**
   Edit what data points and names are visible in the selected chart. See example to right.

Chart filter example

4.2.2 Modify charts

Charts may be selected and modified at any time. Following on the information already provided in this section, here are several examples of chart modifications possible.

A. **Chart Elements:** Turn on data labels and select Outside End for position

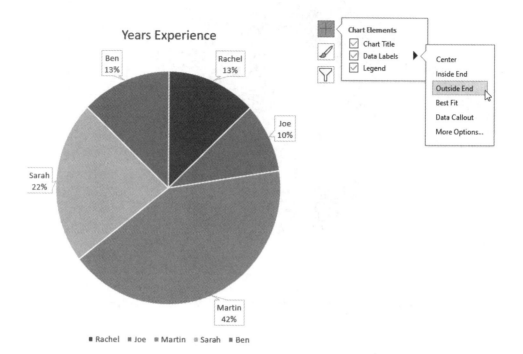

B. **Chart Styles:** Change to another style; **Style 10** in this example

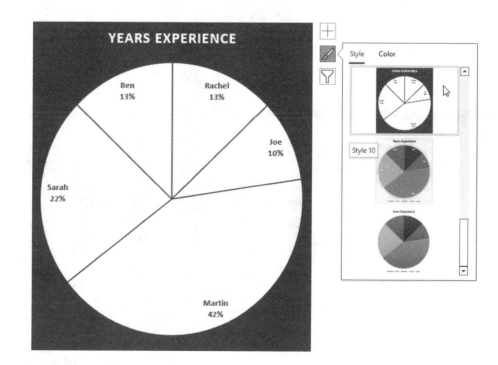

C. **Chart Filter:** Remove a category from the chart, Joe in this example

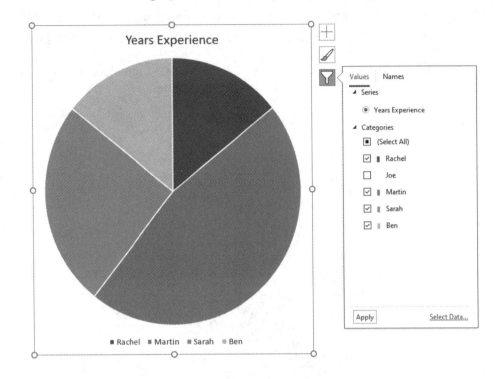

D. **Change Chart Type:** Change from pie to bar, for example.

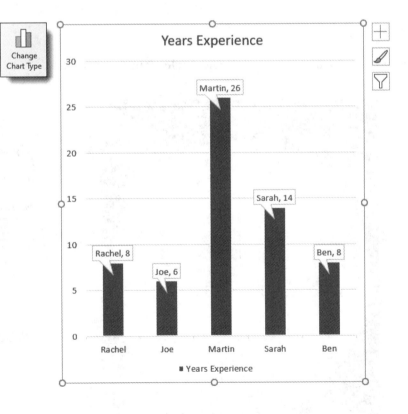

4.3 Insert and format SmartArt graphics

Microsoft created SmartArt, which is supported in multiple Office applications, to facilitate more sophisticated interconnected graphics. For example, elements may be moved, and the connecting line will automatically update. Additionally, elements can be promoted or demoted within a hierarchy to streamline the editing process.

4.3.0 Introduction

In addition to the information covered in this section, it is helpful to know that the right-click options vary depending on which SmartArt style and/or sub-element is selected.

Various right-click options for SmartArt

4.3.1 Insert SmartArt graphics

Review how to create and manage the interconnected shapes known as SmartArt.

Insert SmartArt: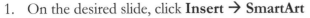

1. On the desired slide, click **Insert → SmartArt**
2. Select an option and click **Insert**
    a. Filter the list by selecting a category on the left
3. Review and/or modify the results

Place a SmartArt element

Below are two additional styles for reference:

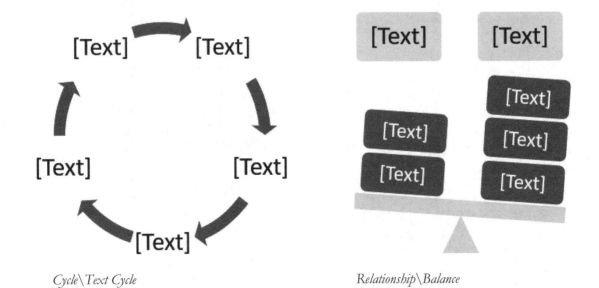

Cycle\Text Cycle   *Relationship\Balance*

4.3.2 Convert lists to SmartArt graphics

Lists can be converted to graphically interesting SmartArt.

Convert lists to SmartArt graphics:

1. Select a list
2. Right-click, and select **Convert to SmartArt**, and then select an option
3. Review the results

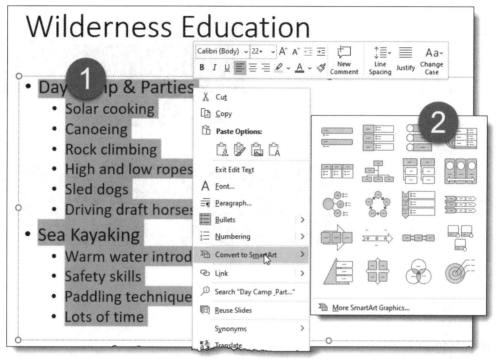

Convert a list to SmartArt graphics

Result of list converted to SmartArt – with optional stock photos added

4.3.3 Add and modify SmartArt graphic content

Review the ways in which SmartArt might be formatted.

Format SmartArt graphics:

4. Select the SmartArt graphic you wish to modify
5. Click **arrow** grip on the left side
6. Edit the text or right-click for more options

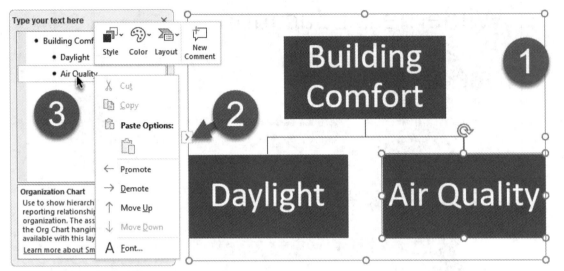

Format SmartArt graphics

Format Tab (on the Ribbon):

With the text selected, in the SmartArt text dialog, the following options are possible:

- **WordArt Styles:** Styles, Text Fill, Text Outline, Text Effects

With a SmartArt, or sub-component selected, the following options are possible:

- **Shape Styles:** Styles, Shape Fill, Shape Outline, Shape Effects
- **Accessibility:** Alt Text (for the visually impaired)
- **Arrange:** Position, Wrap Text, Align, Group, Rotate
- **Size:** Width, and Height

> Shape styles, effects, etc. have names (hover to see via tooltip). Be sure to look for the correct name when provided in the exam.

SmartArt Design Tab (on the Ribbon):

With SmartArt selected, the Layout, Style may be changed as well as resetting the graphic.

Add a SmartArt Shape:

1. Select a SmartArt sub-element
2. Click **SmartArt Design → Add Shape → Add Shape Below**
3. Review the results

Notice the previous are now smaller to allow the new shape to fit in the same bounding area. Click and drag a corner grip to scale the graphic (hold the Shift key to lock the proportions).

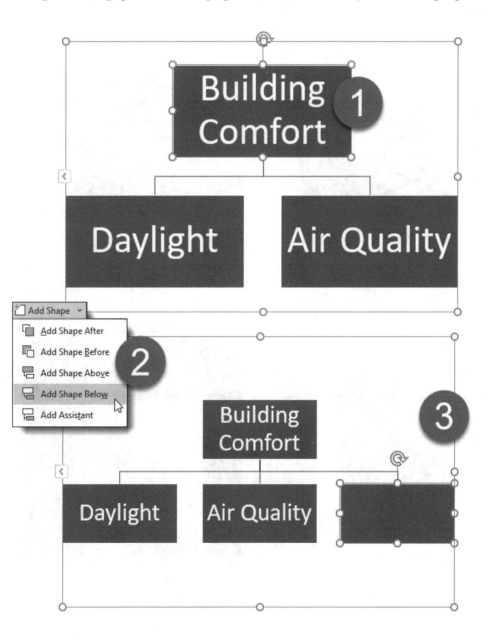

4.4 Insert and modify 3D models

Learn about loading and modifying interactive 3D models within your presentation.

4.4.0 Introduction

This section will show an exciting interactive feature which facilitates loading a 3D model into your presentation. Below are four views of the same 3D model, as an example.

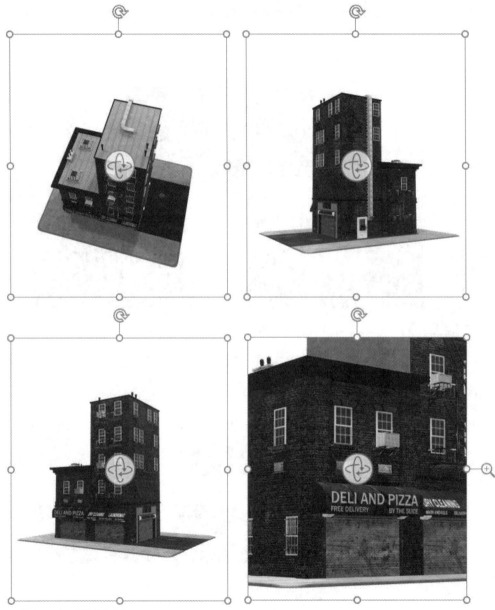

Interactive 3D Model

4.4.1 Insert 3D models

Know how to place and adjust a 3D model within a document.

Insert 3D Models:

1. On the desired slide, **Insert → 3D Models** from online sources
2. Browse for a 3D model to insert and click **Insert**
3. Review the results (see modification steps on next page)

Placing a 3D Model

Adjusting the 3D Model view can be achieved in the following ways:

- Click and drag the **orbit icon** in the center of the graphic when the element is selected.

- Select the 3D Model, then click one of the preset views listed on the 3D Model tab, on the ribbon.

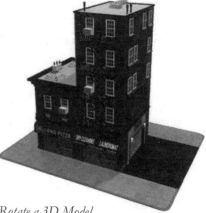

Rotate a 3D Model

4.4.2 Modify 3D models

Once placed, 3D Models have several formatting options available.

Format 3D Models:

1. Select the 3D Model you wish to modify
2. Click **3D Model** on the Ribbon or click and drag the **orbit grip**

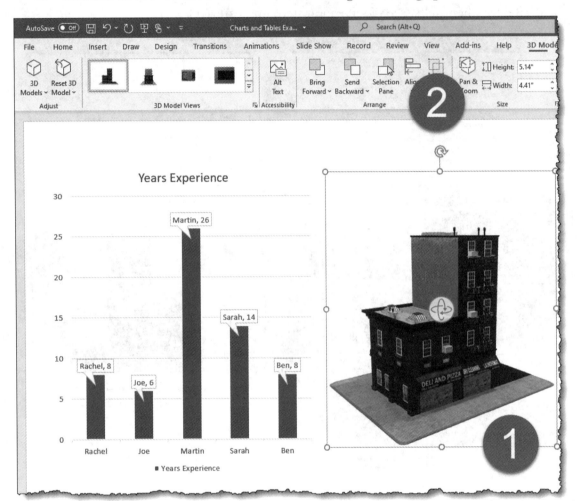

Format 3D Models

With the 3D Model selected, the following options are available:

- **Adjust:** Select a new 3D model or reset to initial/default settings
- **3D Model Views:** Select a pre-defined view (e.g. front, top, etc.)
- **Accessibility:** Alt Text (for the visually impaired)
- **Arrange:** Position, Align, Group
- **Size:** Pan and Zoom, Width, Height

4.5 Insert and manage media

To liven up presentations, it is possible to place video and audio files. This section describes the steps to insert, modify, and -- in some cases -- even create content.

4.5.0 Introduction

Video and audio content can enhance the overall presentation experience for your audience. In some cases, it can even facilitate giving the entire presentation, if the presenter is having technical issues or not feeling well. However, restraint is often needed to avoid overdoing the use of content that might be distracting or impedes your audience from understanding what the presenter is saying.

Like any other assets within a presentation, when a video/audio clip is selected there are several options on the ribbon to control how the content is displayed and played.

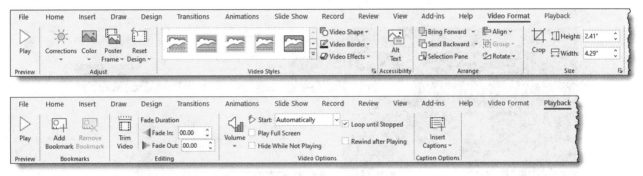

Video format and playback tools on the ribbon

When a video or audio clip is selected, the scale and rotation grips are displayed, as shown to the right.

A playback control bar is also displayed. This facilitates playing the video, fast forward/rewind, and muting the audio.

A computer must have properly configured speakers and a microphone to fully benefit from the features covered in this section.

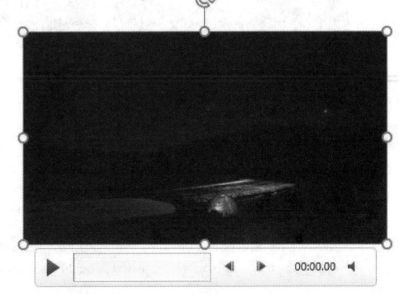

Playback controls for selected video

4.5.1 Insert audio and video clips

Learn the steps required to add a video or audio clip to a presentation.

Insert Video Clip:

1. On the desired slide, click Insert → Video (drop-down) → Stock Videos
2. Select a video and click Insert
   a. Optional, type topic names to search for
3. Adjust size and position of video as needed
   a. Click and drag to move
   b. Click and drag corner grips to resize
   c. Click the Play icon to review the video content

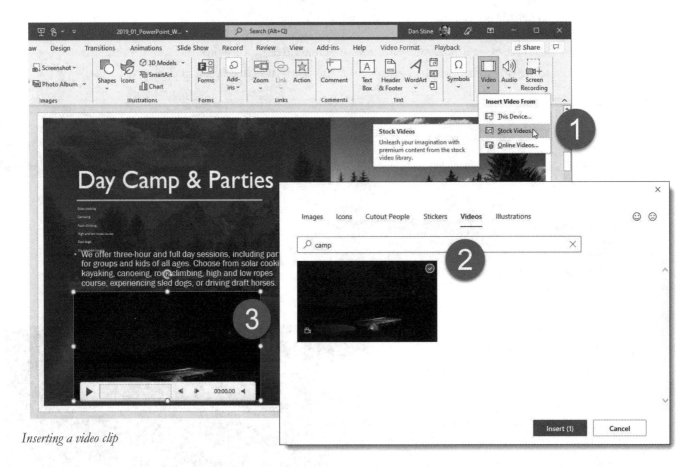

Inserting a video clip

When placing your own videos, located on This Device, many of the standard video formats are supported, such as MP4 and MOV. Note that video files may substantially increase the size of a presentation. Large files can be hard to distribute and depending on the computer displaying the presentation, the playback quality may suffer.

Insert Audio Clip:

1. On the desired slide, click Insert → Audio (drop-down) → Audio on My PC…
2. Select an audio file and click Insert
   a. Browse to the location the file is saved on your computer
3. Adjust the position of the audio graphic as needed
   a. Click and drag to move
   b. Click the Play icon to listen to the audio content (speakers required)

Inserting an audio clip

Both audio and video clips are embedded within the presentation. Thus, they have no connection to the original source files. Any modification made to the original files will not have any effect on the inserted content within the presentation.

4.5.2 Create and insert screen recordings

Learn the steps required to record the screen and insert the results into a presentation.

Create and insert a screen recording:

1. On the desired slide, click Insert → Screen Recording
2. Select an area of the screen to record
   a. Click and drag to select an area
3. Click Record to start recording
   a. Optional: toggle Audio and Record Pointer as desired
4. Press Windows Key + Shift + Q

The result is a video clip placed on the current slide. Be sure to note the key combination to stop recording the screen as it cannot be stopped any other way, short of a computer reboot.

Creating and inserting a screen recording

4.5.3 Configure media playback options

Once a media clip is placed in a presentation, there are several options to control how and when the content is seen or heard by your audience.

Configure video playback:

1. Select a previously placed media clip within your presentation
2. Adjust the Video Options on the ribbon:
   a. **Video**: Low, Medium, High, Mute
   b. **Start**: In Click Sequence, Automatically, When Clicked On
   c. **Play Full Screen**: Fill screen when playing
   d. **Hide while not playing**: Auto play and loop can counter this setting
   e. **Loop until Stopped**: Repeats content rather than playing just once
   f. **Rewind after Playing**: Revert to first frame when stopped

Video playback options

When media is set to start automatically, the content will start immediately during a presentation, when the slide with the content is displayed. If the slide has more than one media item, consider using one of the other start options: In Click Sequence or When Clicked On.

Configure Audio playback:

Audio content have similar options to what was just described above. Notice audio can also play across slides. Selecting the Play in Background audio style sets various audio options: auto start, play across slides, and loop until stopped.

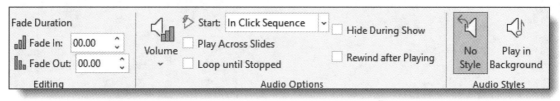

Audio playback options

4.6 Practice tasks

Try the topics covered in this chapter to make sure you understand the concepts. These tasks are sequential and should be completed in the same Word document unless noted otherwise. Saving the results is optional, unless assigned by an instructor.

First Step:

✓ Open provided document **Chapter 4 Assignment.pptx**

Task 1.1:

✓ On the second slide, create a table to match the one shown. Set the table style to **Medium Style 2 – Accent 1**.

Task 1.2

✓ On the third slide, insert any 3D model, from the provided **Stock 3D Models…**, and adjust the 3D view to be different than the default.

Task 1.3

✓ On the fourth slide, create a **pie chart** using the data shown on the slide.

Task 1.4:

✓ On the fifth slide, create any **SmartArt** with at least four objects.

Task 1.5:

✓ On the last slide, insert a **Stock Video**. Adjust its size and location so the existing title text is visible, and set the video to play **full screen**.

4.7 Self-exam & review questions

Self-Exam:

The following questions can be used to check your knowledge of this chapter. The answers can be found at the bottom of the next page.

1. Tables can help maintain content formatting. (T/F)
2. A pie chart cannot be changed to a bar chart. (T/F)
3. Microsoft provides many 3D models online. (T/F)
4. What can be described as interconnected graphics ? _____.
5. Inserting video clips do not increase the presentation file size. (T/F)

Review Questions:

The following questions may be assigned by your instructor to assess your knowledge of this chapter. Your instructor has the answers to the review questions.

1. Columns cannot be deleted from a table. (T/F)
2. Once created, chart categories cannot be hidden. (T/F)
3. A list can be converted to SmartArt. (T/F)
4. The view of a 3D model is changed by dragging on the Orbit Grip. (T/F)
5. During playback, a video can fill the entire screen. (T/F)
6. Video content cannot be rotated. (T/F)
7. Command to stop a screen recording? _____ .
8. Tables can have formulas added, similar to Word and Excel. (T/F)
9. To insert another item into SmartArt, use the Add Shape command. (T/F)
10. PowerPoint can create a video of your computer's desktop. (T/F)

Notes:

5 Apply Transitions and Animations

Introduction

Review essential aspects of Word: navigation, formatting, saving and inspecting documents.

5.0 Consistency and moderation

5.0.0 Finding the right balance when using transitions and animations

As this section will cover, PowerPoint offers several ways to bring a presentation to life using transition effects between slides and animating content on each slide. These features have the ability to emphasize important points and give the audience something to focus on so they do not lose attention.

As exciting as these features are, and even fun to set up, care must be used to not over do it. A presentation can easily get too busy and distracting. This can result in an audience not remembering the important points of a presentation as they might have been distracted by unnecessary "tricks" in the presentation.

Finding the right balance takes practice and improves with experience. Here are some ways to develop a presentation, in general, and to better refine it for your audience:

- Practice your presentation with the proper constraints, such as total time allotted
- Practice the presentation with a sample audience: co-workers, select customer, etc.
- Record practice presentation and review
- Make changes based on review and internal/external feedback

Live Presentations versus Printed Handouts

Keep in mind that the transitions and animations are only effective when presenting live and not so much when printing or providing the audience a digital copy (e.g. PDF file). In addition to needing to present live, the presentation must also be in Presentation mode.

5.1 Apply and configure slide transitions

This section covers a feature called Transitions. This feature is used to liven up a presentation by adding a special effect when moving from the current slide to the next.

5.1.0 Introduction

At a high level, transitions are simply selected from the Transitions tab, on the ribbon, for the current slide. Once applied, several options and timings may be configured.

Transition tab overview

The range of transition options are shown below. Notice each have a name, which will likely be referenced if taking the certification exam.

Subtle

| None | Morph | Fade | Push | Wipe | Split | Reveal | Cut | Random Bars | Shape | Uncover | Cover | Flash |

Exciting

Fall Over	Drape	Curtains	Wind	Prestige	Fracture	Crush	Peel Off	Page Curl	Airplane	Origami	Dissolve	Checkerboa...
Blinds	Clock	Ripple	Honeycomb	Glitter	Vortex	Shred	Switch	Flip	Gallery	Cube	Doors	Box
Comb	Zoom	Random

Dynamic Content

| Pan | Ferris Wheel | Conveyor | Rotate | Window | Orbit | Fly Through |

Transition options

5.1.1 Apply basic and 3D slide transitions

A slide transition presents an engaging effect while moving from the current slide to the next.

Apply basic slide transition:

1. Select one or more slide thumbnails on the left
    a. Use Shift + Select to select all slides back to current slide
    b. Use Ctrl + Select to select multiple non-sequential slides
2. On the Transitions tab, select a transition to apply to the selected slides
    a. Basic transition: a simple fade or slide effect
    b. 3D transition: a 3D effect where previous and current slides are mapped to moving surfaces

When a transition is applied to a single slide, the effect happens upon viewing that slide (i.e. moving from a previous slide to this one). Notice a small start icon appears next to the thumbnail, as pointed out. This indicates the slide contains a transition or media element.

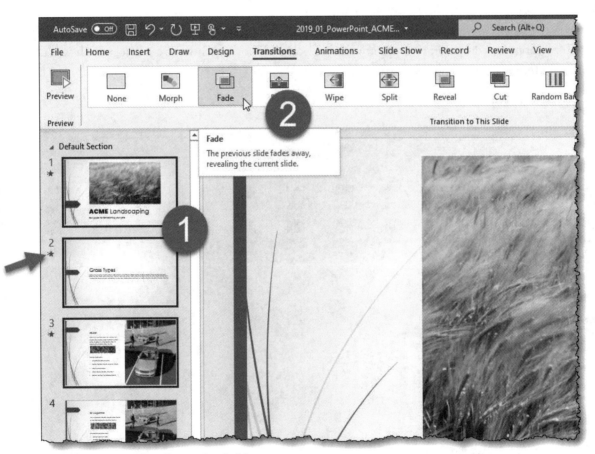

Applying a transition effect to selected slides

5.1.2 Configure transition effects

Once a transition has been applied to a slide, there are several configurable options.

Configure slide transition effects:

1. Select a slide thumbnail on the left
   a. Note: selecting more than one slide can limit editable options
2. Adjust one or more of the following settings:
   a. Effect Options:
      - Options shown vary by transition
      - Example shown: change the direction the 'Cover' transition occurs
   b. Timing options, see additional information below.

Configuring slide transition effects

Timing options range from the duration of the transition to show how long a slide is displayed. Thus, with these settings an entire presentation could be automated to help stay on track.

- **Sound:** Play selected sound
- **Duration:** Transition timing
- **Apply to All:** Current settings applied to entire presentation

- Advance Slide
  - **One Mouse Click:** Transition on click, or 'After' time listed below
  - **After:** Length of time to show current slide

5.2 Animate slide content

Animating content on a slide can help draw attention to important aspects of a presentation.

5.2.0 Introduction

Individual text and graphic elements may be animated. This usually means they are not visible at first, and then make a noticeable entrance by flying across the slide or glowing and turning into existence.

The animation styles and options, from the Animations tab, are expanded below. The "More" options shown at the bottom are more advanced settings not fully covered in this book, but self-exploration is encouraged (tip: search Help for more information).

Animation styles and options

5.2.1 Animate text and graphic elements

Individual elements can be made to move and/or fade into the current slide.

Animate text and graphic elements:

1. Select a text or graphic element to be animated
2. On the Animations tab, select an animation style

When an animation is applied, a preview of the animation automatically occurs. To see the animation again, click the Preview button on the Animations tab.

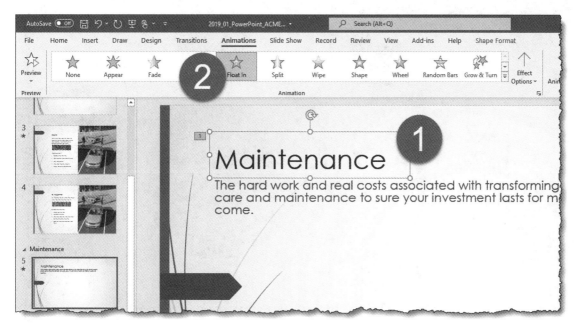

Animating text

This example shows the steps required to animate text. The steps are similar for graphic elements. Notice animations are numbered in the order created on each slide (more on this later in this section). These numbers are hidden while in presentation mode.

5.2.2 Animate 3D models

3D models can be made to animate.

Animate 3D models: 🎥

1. Select a 3D model to be animated
2. On the Animations tab, select an animation style

When an animation is applied, a preview of the animation automatically occurs. To see the animation again, click the Preview button on the Animations tab.

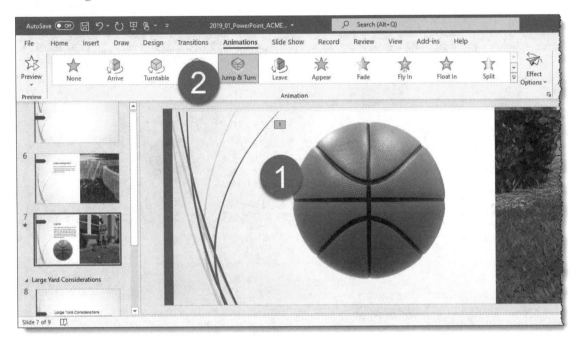

Animating 3D models

In this example, Jump & Turn animation is applied to a basketball (3D Model); the animation first compresses the ball and then jumps it up over the adjacent text, while also spinning the ball. The image below tries to capture this in the printed book.

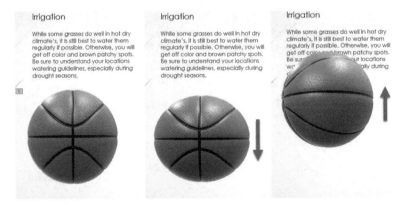

Still images of animated 3D model, start, compressed, and jump/turn

5.2.3 Configure animation effects

Once an animation has been applied to a slide, there are several configurable options.

Configure slide animation effects:

1. Select the animated elements to modify
2. Adjust one or more of the following settings:
    a. Effect Options:
        - Options shown vary by animation style and selection
        - Example shown: Sequence 'By Paragraph' which causes multiple animation sequences within the same element (e.g. text box)
    b. Timing options, see additional information below.

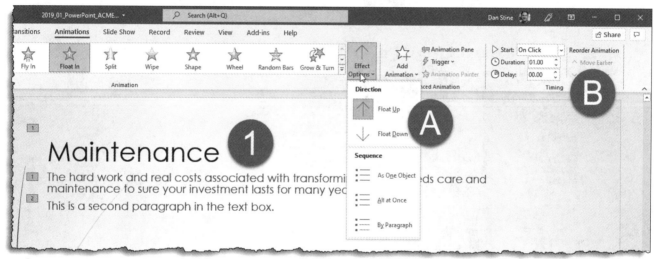

Configuring slide animation effects

Timing options range from the duration of the amination to position in sequence (when other animations exist on the same slide).

- **Start:** On Click, With Previous, After Previous
- **Duration:** Animation length
- **Delay:** Time to delay animation start

- Reorder Animation
  - **Move Earlier:** Play earlier in sequence on slide
  - **Move Later:** Play later in sequence on slide

5.2.4 Configure animation paths

Once an animation has been applied to a slide, the path may be modified.

Configure animation path: 🎥

1. Select the animated element to modify
2. On the Animations tab, select a path option: Turns in this example
3. Optional: Select Effect Options → Reverse Path Direction

Notice, when the animated element is selected that path is shown. It is also possible to click and drag on the start and end grips to further adjust the path.

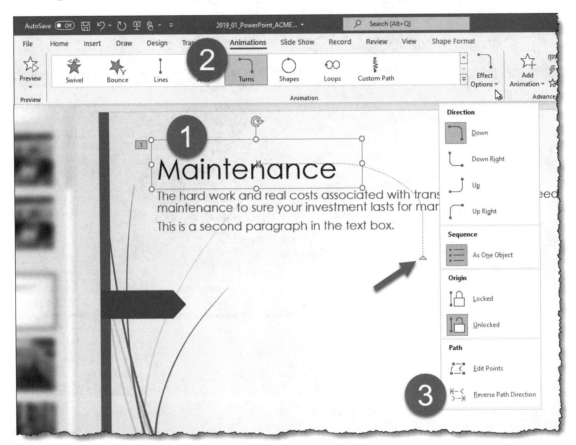

Configuring the animation path

For additional motion paths, expand the animation styles drop-down and select **More Motion Paths…** This opens a dialog, partially shown to the right, with a wide range of path options.

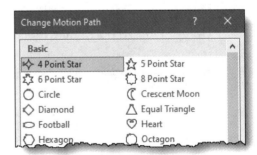

More motion path options

5.2.5 Reorder animations on a slide

When a slide has multiple animations, the sequent (or order) in which the animations happen can be adjusted.

Reorder animations on a slide:

1. On the desired slide, select Animations → Animation Pane
2. In the Animation Pane, click and drag items to change their order
3. Review the results

Use the Preview tool, on the Animation tab, to verify the results are as intended.

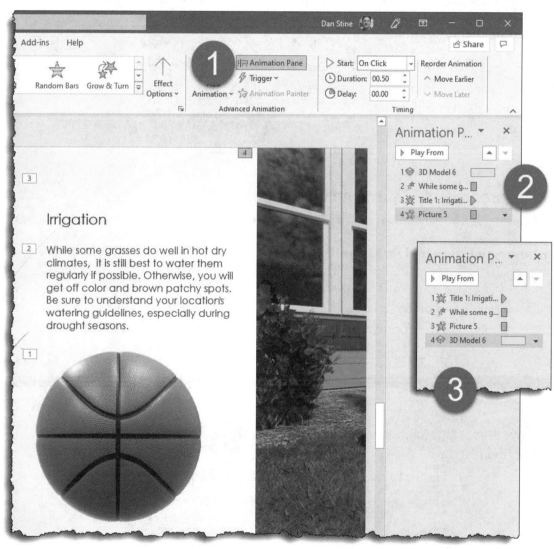

Reordering animation sequence on a slide

Setting the **Start** option to **With Previous** allows two elements to animate simultaneously.

5.3 Set timing for transitions

Transitions and animations have several options and timings which may be modified.

5.3.0 Introduction

This section will cover the steps to set the timing for a selected slide.

5.3.1 Set transition effect duration

The time it takes for a transition to occur can be adjusted using the Duration option.

Set the transition effect duration:

1. On a slide with transition applied, adjust the duration on the Transitions tab.

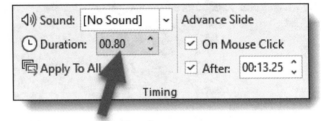

Adjusting transition duration

5.3.2 Configure transition start and finish options

The start and end points of an animation may be modified.

Configure animation start and finish options:

1. Right click on start or end point
2. Select Edit Points
3. Drag point to relocate it

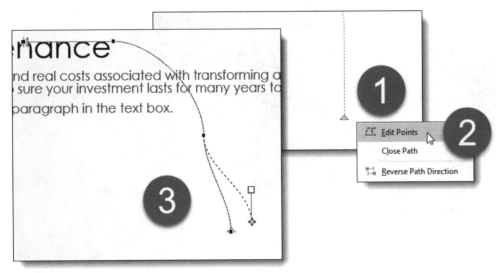

Configure animation start and finish options

5.4 Practice tasks

Try the topics covered in this chapter to make sure you understand the concepts. These tasks are sequential and should be completed in the same Word document unless noted otherwise. Saving the results is optional, unless assigned by an instructor.

First Step:

- ✓ Open provided document **Chapter 5 Assignment.pptx**

Task 1.1:

- ✓ Select slides 2-6 and set transition style to **Uncover**.

Task 1.2

- ✓ On slide 2, animate the text using **Teeter**.

Task 1.3

- ✓ On slide 3, insert a 3D Model and set the animation style to **Jump & Turn**.

Task 1.4:

- ✓ On slide 4, reorder the animations in this order: Tree, Acorn, Text.

Task 1.5:

- ✓ On slide 5, adjust the transition duration to 2.00.

5.5 Self-exam & review questions

Self-Exam:

The following questions can be used to check your knowledge of this chapter. The answers can be found at the bottom of the next page.

1. Transitions can be applied to more than one slide at a time. (T/F)
2. Animation styles are named. (T/F)
3. 3D models cannot be animated. (T/F)
4. Command to list animations on current slide? _____.
5. An animation path can be modified. (T/F)

Review Questions:

The following questions may be assigned by your instructor to assess your knowledge of this chapter. Your instructor has the answers to the review questions.

1. A 3D transition is a simple fade or slide effect. (T/F)
2. "Twist & Turn" is one of the animation styles available. (T/F)
3. The path of an animation can be reversed. (T/F)
4. Each paragraph, in the same text box, can be animated separately. (T/F)
5. Animation sequence numbers are hidden in Presentation mode. (T/F)
6. 3D transitions do not use the graphics on the slides. (T/F)
7. Feature that controls amount of time a transition occurs? _____.
8. Use care to not use too many transitions and/or animations. (T/F)
9. The order in which animations occur on a slide cannot be modified. (T/F)
10. The start of an animation effect can be delayed. (T/F)

SELF-EXAM ANSWERS:
1 – T, 2 – T, 3 – F, 4 – Animation Pane, 5 – T

6 Practice Exam

Introduction

This chapter will highlight the practice exam software provided with this book, including accessing the exam, Installing, required files, user interface and how to interpret the results. Taking this practice exam, after studying this book, will help ensure a successful result when taking the actual Microsoft Office Specialist Certified Associate exam at a test center.

The practice exam questions are similar, not identical, to the actual exam.

Important Things to Know

Here are a few big picture things you should keep in mind:

- **Practice Exam – First Steps**
    - The practice exam, that comes with this book, is taken on **your own computer**
    - You need to have **PowerPoint installed** and ready to use during the practice exam
    - You must download the practice exam software from SDC Publications
        - See inside-front cover of this book for access instructions
    - **Required PowerPoint files** for the practice exam
        - Files downloaded with practice exam software
        - The practice exam software opens the files when they are needed
    - Note which questions you got wrong, and study those topics

- **Practice Exam - Details**
    - Questions: 35
    - Timed: 50 minutes
    - Passing: 70%
    - Results: Presented upon completion

This practice exam can be taken multiple times. But it is recommended that you finish studying this book before taking the practice exam. There are only 35 questions total, so you don't want to get to a point where all the questions, and their answers, have been memorized. This will not help with the actual exam as they are not the same questions.

This practice exam can be taken multiple times.

Practice Exam Overview

The **practice exam** included with this book can be downloaded from the publisher's website using the **access code** found on the inside-front cover. This is a good way to check your skills prior to taking the official exam, as the intent is to offer similar types of questions in roughly the same format as the formal exam. This practice exam is taken at home, work or school, on your own computer. You must have PowerPoint installed to successfully answer the in-application questions.

This is a test drive for the exam process, including:

- Understanding the test software
- How to mark and return to questions
- Exam question format
- Live in-application steps
- How the results are presented at the exam conclusion

Here is a sample of what the practice exam looks like… note that PowerPoint is automatically opened and positioned directly above the practice exam user interface.

Sample question from included practice exam

Having taken the practice exam can remove some anxiety one may have going into an exam that may positively impact a career search or advancement.

Download and Install the Practice Exam

Follow the instructions on the inside-front cover of this book, using the provided access code to download the practice exam. Once the ZIP file is downloaded you must extract the files into a folder that you create.

Download steps:

- Create a folder on your desktop or C drive, such as **C:\MOS Installer**
- Double-click on the downloaded ZIP file
- Copy all the folders/files from the ZIP file to the newly created folder

To install the practice Exam software on your PC-based computer simply double-click the Setup.exe file in the newly created folder. Follow the prompts on screen to complete the installation. Once complete, the folder you just created, and its contents, may be deleted.

Required PowerPoint Files

The installed practice exam software includes several required PowerPoint files to be used during the exam. For the most part, the software will open the files when they are needed. There are, however, a few questions that require a file be selected and imported. In those cases, the current working folder is changed so the file should be directly accessible when trying to access it.

For the practice exam, the required files are installed automatically.

Starting the Exam

From the Windows Start menu, click the **SDC PowerPoint Practice Exam** icon to start the practice exam. If you have purchased and installed more than one SDC practice exam, select the desired practice exam from the list that appears. At this point, the practice exam opens with the timer running. PowerPoint is also opened, along with the required presentation.

Note the following formatting conventions used in the exam questions:
- **Bold text** is used to indicate file or folder names as well as setting names.
- Clicking on underlined text copies it to the clipboard. Use **Ctrl + V** to paste into PowerPoint to avoid typing errors.
- Text in "quotation marks" represents existing text within the document.

Practice Exam User Interface (UI)

The following image, and subsequent list, highlight the features of the practice exam's user interface.

User Interface details:

- **Menu:** (drop-down list)
    - **About…** – Exam software version information
    - **Float Application Window** – Use to reposition practice exam on the desktop
    - **Dock to Desktop Bottom** – Default option, exam fixed to bottom of screen
    - **Show Status Bar** – Toggle visibility at bottom of screen
    - **Exam Summary** – Review marked questions
    - **Finish Exam…** – Grade the exam
    - **Close** – Closes the Practice Exam and PowerPoint
- **Task Tabs:** Each tab contains a question for the current project and may be marked for review or as completed. Click a tab to view its question or use Previous/Next buttons.
- **Time Remaining:** Time remaining for the 50 minute timed exam
- **Exam Summary:** Review marked questions and return to previous project/question
- **Project Controls:**
    - **Restart Project** – Discards all changes made to the current workbook
    - **Submit Project** – Advance to next project or exam completion on last project
- **Close App:** Closes the Practice Exam and PowerPoint
- **Current Project:** Current project name and number listed for reference on status bar
- **Task Controls:** *for the current project…*
    - **Previous Task** – View the previous task/question
    - **Mark for Review** – *Optional:* When unsure of the answer, mark task for review
    - **Mark as Complete** – *Optional:* When confident, mark the task as complete
    - **Task Help** – *Optional:* Reveal steps required to achieve a correct answer
    - **Next Task** – Advance to the next task/question

When unsure of the correct answer, after multiple attempts, click the **Task Help** button to reveal the steps required to answer the current question. The image below shows an example.

Practice exam - Help example

The following image shows an example of tasks marked for review and as complete. This is optional, and just meant as a way of tracking one's progress. It is possible to advance to the next project without marking any tasks.

Practice exam – Marked task exams

Practice Exam Results

When you complete the practice exam, you will find out if you passed or failed. Be sure to note which questions were answered incorrectly and review those related sections in the book.

Conclusion

As with any formal exam, the more you practice the more likely you are to have successful results. So, be sure to take the time to download the provided practice exam and give it a try before you head off to the testing facility and take the actual exam.

Good luck!

Microsoft Office Specialist – PowerPoint Associate 365/2019 - Exam Preparation
Exam Day Study Guide

> Remembering where the right tools and commands are can be half the battle. Leading up to exam day, use this handy reference sheet to firm up your knowledge of important topics that will help you pass the Word exam.

Reminders

- ✓ Bring **photo ID**
- ✓ Know your Certiport **username** and **password**
- ✓ Bring exam **payment confirmation**
- ✓ Know where the testing center is; e.g. have the **building address**

Tips

- ✓ Carefully read each question
- ✓ If unsure, mark question for review and come back to it later if you have time
- ✓ Click underlined text in question to copy that text to the clipboard
- ✓ Accept all defaults unless otherwise instructed

Commands

- ⬇ **File** tab
  - ✓ Save As, Alternate file formats
  - ✓ Info, Properties, Check for issues
  - ✓ Print, Print settings
  - ✓ Share
- ⬇ **Home** tab
  - ✓ New Slide
  - ✓ Reuse Slides (import from other files)
  - ✓ Layout
  - ✓ Fonts
  - ✓ Font Formatting (Bold, etc.)
  - ✓ Bulleted/Numbered List
  - ✓ Increase/Decrease Indent
  - ✓ Clear All Formatting
  - ✓ Drawing
  - ✓ Find/Replace & Advanced Find
- ⬇ **Insert** tab
  - ✓ Pictures
  - ✓ Screenshot
  - ✓ Shapes
  - ✓ 3D Models
  - ✓ SmartArt
  - ✓ Chart
  - ✓ Links (Zoom, Summary, Section, Slide)
  - ✓ Header & Footer: insert, modify, delete
  - ✓ Text Box
  - ✓ Video
  - ✓ Audio
  - ✓ Screen Recording

- ⬇ **Design** tab
  - ✓ Theme
  - ✓ Slide Size
  - ✓ Format Background
- ⬇ **Transitions** tab
  - ✓ Preview
  - ✓ Transition style
  - ✓ Effect Options
  - ✓ Timing (Sound, Duration, Advance)
- ⬇ **Animations** tab
  - ✓ Preview
  - ✓ Animation styles
  - ✓ Animation Pane (Reorder)
  - ✓ Timing (Start, Duration, Delay, reorder)
- ⬇ **Slide Show** tab
  - ✓ Start Slide Show, From Beginning
  - ✓ Custom Slide Show
  - ✓ Set Up (Presentation Options)
- ⬇ **Review** tab
  - ✓ Spelling
  - ✓ Thesaurus
  - ✓ New Comment
  - ✓ Show Comments
- ⬇ **View** tab
  - ✓ Views, Normal, Outline, etc.
  - ✓ Slide Master
  - ✓ Handout Master
  - ✓ Notes Master

Notes:

Index

SDC PUBLICATIONS **Document Inspector (aka Check for Issues) checks for comments.**	File (tab)
SDC PUBLICATIONS **The presentation Theme cannot be changed while editing the slide master.**	False
SDC PUBLICATIONS **Show Comments is found on which tab?**	Presenter
SDC PUBLICATIONS **How many slides are on a printed Notes page?**	Rehearse Timings
SDC PUBLICATIONS **Which command lets readers know a presentation is final?**	True

SDC PUBLICATIONS **The Create PDF command is found on which tab?**	True
SDC PUBLICATIONS **It is not possible to password protect a presentation.**	False
SDC PUBLICATIONS **View used while delivering a presentation?**	Review
SDC PUBLICATIONS **Command used to make sure you have enough time to deliver a presentation.**	One
SDC PUBLICATIONS **Custom slide shows can be created to leave out certain slides**	Mark as Final

SDC PUBLICATIONS **Slides can be created by importing an outline from Microsoft Word?**	1. Summary 2. Section 3. Slide
SDC PUBLICATIONS **Tool to create an interactive way to navigate a presentation.**	False
SDC PUBLICATIONS **To reorder slides, simply draw their thumbnail in Normal view.**	True
SDC PUBLICATIONS **Command, on Insert tab, to extract a slide from another presentation.**	Insert
SDC PUBLICATIONS **Slide layouts can only be selected after creating a new slide.**	Section

SDC PUBLICATIONS **List the three types of Zoom Slides**	True
SDC PUBLICATIONS **It is not possible to duplicate a slide.**	Summary Zoom Slide
SDC PUBLICATIONS **Hiding a slide only hides it during a presentation.**	True
SDC PUBLICATIONS **Which tab is the Header & Footer command found on?**	Reuse Slides
SDC PUBLICATIONS **What is the command/feature that groups slides together?**	False

SDC PUBLICATIONS Feature that causes multiple elements to move together?	False
SDC PUBLICATIONS Feature used to position elements relative to each other	Ctrl + C
SDC PUBLICATIONS 'Bring to Front' places the selected element on all other elements.	True
SDC PUBLICATIONS Feature that contains text.	Home
SDC PUBLICATIONS Shapes can contain text.	Screenshot

SDC PUBLICATIONS	
Picture effects permanently modify the selected image.	Group
SDC PUBLICATIONS Keyboard shortcut to copy the selected element to the clipboard.	Align
SDC PUBLICATIONS PowerPoint Themes control much of the formatting in a presentation.	True
SDC PUBLICATIONS On which tab is the Add/Remove Columns tool found?	Text Box
SDC PUBLICATIONS Command to Insert the full view of another application, currently open, on the current slide.	True

SDC PUBLICATIONS **What helps maintain formatting when text needs to be in rows and columns?**	Windows Key + Shift + Q
SDC PUBLICATIONS **Individual rows can be deleted from tables**	True
SDC PUBLICATIONS **A list can be converted to SmartArt**	False
SDC PUBLICATIONS **What other Microsoft Office app, containing an outline, can be used to create slides?**	• In Click Sequence • Automatically • When Clicked On
SDC PUBLICATIONS **What command is used to insert another item into SmartArt?**	True

SDC PUBLICATIONS	
Command to stop a screen recording?	Tables
PowerPoint can create a video of your computer's desktop.	True
Inserting videos into a presentation does not make the file larger.	True
Name the three options available for starting a video.	Microsoft Word
The title of a chart can be turned off (hidden)	Add Shape

SDC PUBLICATIONS **Transitions can only be applied to one slide at a time.**	True
SDC PUBLICATIONS **3D transitions map the two slides onto animated surfaces.**	False
SDC PUBLICATIONS **Once modified, the path of an animation cannot be reset.**	True
SDC PUBLICATIONS **Name the feature that controls the amount of time it takes for a transition to occur.**	Animation Pane
SDC PUBLICATIONS **Too many transition styles can be distracting.**	Reverse Path Direction

SDC PUBLICATIONS **Each animation style has a name.**	False
SDC PUBLICATIONS **3D models cannot be animated.**	True
SDC PUBLICATIONS **Each paragraph, in the same text box, can be animated separately.**	False
SDC PUBLICATIONS **Name the command that opens a list of animations, lists the order and allows them to be rearranged.**	Duration
SDC PUBLICATIONS **Name the command used to flip the direction of an animation.**	True